Evangelistic Sermons

JAMES P. WESBERRY

Evan-gelistic Sermons

BROADMAN PRESS
Nashville, Tennessee

ISBN: 0-8054-2220-X
4222-20

Library of Congress Catalog Card Number: 73-80775
Dewey Decimal Classification: 243
Printed in the United States of America

To
My Wife
SUE
who has greatly
inspired and
encouraged me

Foreword

Evangelistic Sermons by Dr. James Wesberry, is a most helpful series of messages. Many things converge to make this so.

The book is both Christ-centered and person-centered. From first to last, it is permeated with the person of Jesus Christ. It is also sensitive to man's deepest and most profound needs. It reflects the author's interest into broad areas which affect people's lives.

The book is evangelistic. The shepherd heart of Dr. Wesberry reveals itself in every paragraph. In his years as pastor he has been equally at home while praying with a political leader or helping a child to know Jesus Christ. Very few books are as readable as this one. While the material is clear, it is also profound. Dr. Wesberry is a master at illustration and draws from both broad experience and wide reading. Each chapter is a well-lighted house with every idea illuminated and applied to life.

More than anything else, there is a directness and warmth that persuade men "in Christ's name be ye reconciled."

Kenneth L. Chafin

Houston, Texas

Contents

Introduction

One of the greatest needs of the generation in which we live is a sane, strong, stalwart evangelism on the part of ministers. About the most tragic thing imaginable would be a ministry devoid of passion for souls. Such a ministry has missed its mark and is a pitiable failure, no matter how popular or famous it may be. The minister is indeed fortunate who is handsome, winsome, attractive, cultured, gifted in speech, a strong pulpiteer, a good mixer, a great administrator, a mighty builder, a humble, faithful, consecrated pastor; but, next to his relationship to Christ, it seems to me that above all else he must know, love, and seek untiringly the salvation of lost souls. What does it matter if he have the strength of an ox, the tenacity of a bulldog, the vision of an eagle, the melodies of a nightingale, the meekness of a lamb, the daring of a lion, the patience of a donkey, the industry of a beaver, the versatility of a chameleon, the hide of a rhinocerous, the resignation of the incurable, the loyalty of an apostle, the tenderness of a shepherd, the devotion of a mother if he have not the fervency of the evangelist?

Christianity was launched on a wave of evangelism. It was Christ's intent that Christianity should cover the earth as the waters cover the sea. He dreamed of world conquest, and he himself was the preeminent lover of souls, the ideal soulwinner of the ages.

Dr. W. T. Derieux, Secretary of the South Carolina Convention, once advised that every young minister read 1 and 2

Timothy once a week. For in 2 Timothy 4:5 Paul says: "Watch thou in all things, endure afflictions, do the work of an evangelist, make full proof of thy ministry." It is in this spirit that I offer this book of sermons to soul-winners in every walk of life. In the words of one of the most beloved preachers of all times:

Happy if with my latest breath
I may but speak His name;
Preach Him to all, and gasp in death,
Behold, behold the Lamb!

1.
God's Greatest Gift

JOHN 3:14-17

"For God so loved the world, that he gave his only begotten Son, that whosoever believeth in him should not perish, but have everlasting life" (v. 16).

The Bible is more than any man has ever said of it. The Bible is more than all men together have said of it or can say of it. The Bible is God's book. It is a divine-human book, a Holy Spirit-inspired book. No man can ever say enough about the Bible.

When Sir Walter Scott was on his deathbed, he said to his son-in-law, "Read me from the book." His son-in-law asked, "From what book?" And Sir Walter Scott said: "Need you ask? There is but one book. Read me from that book."

When John Wanamaker was a little boy, he spent $2.75 for a red Bible. Years later some of his transactions earned him millions of dollars, but he said that never in all his life had he made a greater investment than that $2.75 spent for a red Bible.

William Lyon Phelps of Yale University, a great man of literature, said that if he had to choose between the knowledge provided by a college education and the knowledge gleaned from the Bible, he would always choose the knowledge of the Bible.

The Bible speaks for itself.

The word "Bible" comes from the Latin which means little books. The Bible is a collection of sixty-six books, thirty-nine in the Old Testament and twenty-seven in the New. If something were to happen to every one of the books of the Old Testament, and to every one of the books of the New Testament but one, and then if something were to happen to every chapter in that book save one chapter, and to every verse in that chapter save one verse, there would still be enough left for us to know the story of God's redeeming love!

That one verse is known as the gospel in a nutshell, as the golden text of the Bible, as the lens of the whole revelation of God, as the diamond of the Scriptures. That great verse of Scripture summarizes for us all that we need to know about God. The verse does what John Milton tried to do for us in a poem and was unable to do. He tried to write a poem on the cross and failed. He said: "I will try no more. It is a never-ebbing sea in which our thoughts are drowned." Neither speech, drama, art, music, nor anything else can fully express the glory of the cross.

This verse of Scripture summarizes for us the meaning of the cross. It contains eleven superlatives:

"For God" — the greatest lover;
"so loved" — the greatest degree;
"the world" — the greatest company;
"that he gave" — the greatest act;
"his only begotten Son" — the greatest gift;
"that whosoever" — the greatest opportunity;
"believeth" — the greatest simplicity;
"on him" — the greatest attraction;
"should not perish" — the greatest promise;
"but" — the greatest difference;
"have everlasting life" — the greatest possibility.

An Ancient Love

One day I saw a man on his knees, his head shaved in preparation for electrocution. He had committed a terrible crime, and now he was paying the penalty for his crime. There he was on bended knee, praying his last prayer before the iron door would swing open and he would walk down the corridor into the death room itself, sit down in the death chair, and be electrocuted. I saw a man pull the lever, and I saw the man flinch; and in one minute and forty-three seconds he was dead. I smelled the odor which came from his burned body, and I left that room nauseated and sick, not only because of that odor, but also because of sin and the penalty of sin for man.

But I shall never forget a placard at the head of the cot where the man knelt. In contrast to what another prisoner wrote on a cell wall at old Rock Quarry Prison of Incorrigibles in Georgia — "There ain't no God" — on this black placard, symbolic of the blackness of sin, were these words in letters of red, symbolic of the shed blood of Jesus Christ: "God is love." *God is love!* Those three little words summarize John 3:16.

There is a conception of God which is *not* love. Some people think of God as a God of anger, a God of wrath. They think of him as a cruel monster in the sky. Some think of him as having a whip in his hand, waiting angrily for the sinner to come home. One of the greatest preachers of America, Jonathan Edwards, went up and down the land preaching a sermon he titled "Sinners in the Hands of an Angry God."

There are those who think about God as a God of retaliation, a God of revenge, a God of hate, a God of war. But the God I know is a God whose very name is love. A song has these words by an unknown author:

Could we with ink the ocean fill,
And were the skies of parchment made;
Were ev'ry stalk on earth a quill,
And ev'ry man a scribe by trade;
To write the love of God above
Would drain the ocean dry;
Nor could the scroll contain the whole,
Tho' stretched from sky to sky.

Let us think about the antiquity of God's love. The psalmist said, "From everlasting to everlasting, thou art God" (90:2). Jesus said, "Thou lovedst me before the foundation of the world" (John 17:24).

Some years ago a Russian discovered a rock estimated to be 1,852,000,000 years of age. I know nothing about the age of rocks; but if you were to ask me about the Rock of Ages, I would tell you about Jesus. I would tell you that before that billion-year-old rock was ever formed, God existed, and he existed as a God whose greatest attribute is that of holy love. Before the mountains were ever piled, before this world was ever created, he existed as a God of love whose love is from everlasting unto everlasting.

A Constant Love

Let us think, too, about the constancy of God's love. How unfaithful some people are, how untrustworthy! But God's love is the same yesterday, today, and forever; it never changes. Man's love may change. Man may forsake God, but God never forsakes man. He will never let man go; his love will never let man down. God loves man to the very brink of hell itself.

A woman came to my office one day and sat and talked for an hour. She told me that after less than one month of marriage, she discovered that her husband was unfaithful. Across the twenty-five years of their marriage, there had been a succession of women. And she asked me what she should do.

It was a tragic story, and for the first time in my life that I can remember, I advised divorce. Then she said to me: "Well, I know you're right, preacher. I should have done it a long time ago. But I have been hoping and praying that someday God would speak to him, and he would be gloriously converted to the man I thought he was when I married him. I love him so much!"

How beautiful is a love like that. It is reminiscent of an Old Testament love story. Hosea came home one day to find his three little children all alone there, and he asked, "Where's Mother?" They answered, "She went off with another man today and said she won't be back." The years rolled by, and one day when this woman had plumbed the depths of sin and shame and was being sold as a slave on the slave block, Hosea purchased her and carried her back to be the mother of his children.

God's love is like that. He loves you and me like that. There is nothing so great, so comforting, so helpful, so uplifting, so inspiring, or so ennobling as the love of God.

A long time ago I decided that as long as my mother lived, I would do everything I knew how for her so that when she passed on, I would have as few regrets as possible. Among the sweetest memories that linger in my mind are the memories of having walked with her in the footsteps of Jesus — of having gone to the little town of Bethlehem to the place below the ground where they say Jesus was actually born, and where his body lay; to Nazareth, to the Sea of Galilee, to Jerusalem, and to the hill of Calvary.

On the night that she lay dying in Georgia Baptist Hospital, I stood by her bedside and told the nurse how my mother and I had gone to these sacred places together. I could feel my mother's pulse quicken, and I saw a radiant look upon her face as she thought about walking there with Christ.

After she passed on I buried her body beside the body of my dad, who had been killed in a tragic automobile accident some twenty-five or thirty years earlier, and then I went to their home. As I looked over her possessions, I found her Bibles — she had five or six — and I gathered them up and began to look through them. On the flyleaf of every Bible I found my picture.

I didn't know anyone had ever loved me like that. I could truly say with Kipling,

> If I were hanged on the highest hill,
> Mother o' mine, Mother o' mine,
> I know whose love would follow me still,
> Mother o' mine, Mother o' mine.

But as sweet and as great as a mother's love can be, there is a love that is ten million times greater, and that is God's love for you and me. Yes, we are the objects of God's love! You and I love those who are lovely; you and I love those who love us. But God loves even those who do not love him. God loves those who are not so lovely. He loves the saint and the sinner, the good and the bad. No man anywhere has ever gone so far in sin but that he is the object of God's great love. No woman has ever been so soiled in character but that she, too, is the object of God's love.

One day the Pharisees brought a woman to Jesus. They cared nothing for the poor woman; they were merciless. They were thinking only of themselves. They said to Jesus, "Master, this woman was taken in adultery, in the very act. Now Moses in the law commanded us, that such should be stoned; but what sayest thou" (John 8:4-5)? And Jesus stooped over and with his finger wrote on the ground as though he had not heard them. He was silent. They pressed him for a reply. And his calm, clear voice was heard above the clamoring noise of the throng as he said: "He that is without sin among you, let him first cast a stone at her" (v. 7). And they hung their heads in shame and skulked away like demons. Then Jesus looked into the face of that poor, brokenhearted woman and said, "Woman, where are those thine accusers? hath no man condemned thee? . . . Neither do I condemn thee: go, and sin no more" (vv. 10-11).

Poor, broken, bleeding, benighted humanity has never had such a friend as Jesus Christ. They referred to him as the friend of sinners. They thought they were being sarcastic, but actually they had never paid him a higher compliment. He is the best friend any poor sinner ever had.

In New York City there is a quaint little church favored by actors and actresses called the "Church Around the Corner." On the wall hang paintings of many of these famous people. The story of how this unique church got its name is told in a book entitled *I Went to Church in New York City*. Upon the death of an actor named George Holland, a friend of his, Joseph Jefferson, went to one of the fashionable churches on Fifth Avenue and asked the preacher if they could have the funeral service there. The pastor refused and directed him to the little church around the corner. And Jefferson said, "May God bless the little church around the corner."

Every church ought to be the little church around the corner, the sinner's friend. For when any man comes to the end of the road, the end of that road ought to be an open church door where he may find the grace of God, the redeeming love of the Savior. For God so loved the world — the whole wide world and everybody in it — that he gave.

A Perfect Love

Love gives and gives and gives. Love is unselfish; love never hoards; love expends itself; love is sacrificial. God so loved the world that he gave his gold, his diamonds, and his silver to make it a world of great material resources. But more than that, God gave his only begotten Son. Someone has said, "If I had been God, I might have gone myself, but I could never have sent my son." Whoever said that did not understand the full meaning of the cross. For God was in Christ, reconciling the world unto himself. And the nails that pierced the hands of Jesus went through the hands of God. God never suffered more than when Christ died upon the cross for the sins of the world.

A colonel in the United States Air Force was speaking enthusiastically of all the trouble the government had gone to in trying to locate a major who was lost in flight. He doubted if there had ever been such a search made for any man. Planes were sent in from many thousands of miles away to join in the search. They exploded ten thousand lights, and one plane and one life were lost in the search. The colonel explained how valuable one man is to Uncle Sam and went on to say that it would not matter what his rank, Uncle Sam would make the same effort. "Just think of it!" he exclaimed. "Ten million dollars for one little man!"

Ten million dollars is a lot of money. But God gave far more than that for *each* of us. He gave his all—his Son, his love, himself—"that whosoever believeth in him should not perish, but have everlasting life." The world had plenty of religions, but it did not have a religion like this. God didn't want us to perish; he didn't want us to go to hell. He wanted to save us, to emancipate us, to forgive us, to deliver us, to bring us a great salvation; and so he gave us that salvation in Christ. And all God demands is that you and I shall return his love, love for love.

An English novelist wrote a book in which there is a lovely woman who marries a man weak of will and evasive of life's larger meanings and responsibilities. One day after many years of happy married life, this man came home shamed and broken and told her that he would have to be taken off to prison in a few days for a crime he'd committed. The news was like an electric shock to her, but when she was finally able to pull herself together, she said to him, "Well, since you and I have committed this crime together, we will share its consequences together." The effect was like a bolt of lightning. He said: "You didn't have anything to do with it! You weren't even aware of it. I've embarrassed you, humiliated you, hurt you. You should never have married me." And then she looked at him with deep and brooding eyes and said: "Is it possible that after all these years of happy wedded life, you do not know that my love for you goes so deep that you cannot commit a deed and I not commit that deed with you? We will face the consequences together."

God is like that. You and I are guilty; God is innocent. You and I are sinful; God is sinless. We are imperfect, but God is perfect. We are the offenders; God is the offended. Yet we see him, offended and innocent, take upon himself that cruel and heavy cross, and go staggering and stumbling up that hill of Calvary. We see the nails driven through his hands; we see him lifted up there between heaven and earth to suffer and bleed and die for our sins — the innocent for the guilty, the good for the bad, the righteous for the unrighteous, the sinless for the sinful, the offended for the offender. God went to the cross to take away our sins, to bear them away from us as far as the East is from the West, to remember them against us no more. God blots out all our sins. No one can see our sins through the blood of Jesus Christ, for the blood of Christ cleanses us from all sin.

When George Matheson of Scotland was a young man, he was desperately in love with a certain young woman and engaged to be married, when a doctor told him he was losing his sight. He knew that he would have to talk to her about it, so he went to her and said: "The doctor tells me I'm going blind. In a few months I won't be able to see, and you don't want to spend the rest of your life leading a blind man around. I want to do the right thing, so I am offering you release from this engagement." She accepted, and his heart was broken, and afterward he wrote these beautiful lines:

O Love that wilt not let me go,
I rest my weary soul in thee;
I give thee back the life I owe,
That in thine ocean depths its flow
May richer, fuller be.

God loves us. All he demands is that we accept his love and love him in return, and eternity will be ours.

2. Going Deeper with God

ACTS 1:4-9

"Ye shall receive power, after that the Holy Ghost is come upon you" (v. 8).

E. Stanley Jones has said that the lost chord in Christianity is Pentecost, and that Pentecost is the land where our resources lie, but lie undeveloped. Certainly we need to find that chord, discover that land, and develop those resources. We need to be filled with God's Holy Spirit.

Jesus told his disciples one day to wait in Jerusalem until they should receive power from on high. They did so, and on the day of Pentecost there came the sound of a rushing wind, and the Holy Ghost filled their presence. And when it did, some mysterious and miraculous things happened, as they always do when the Holy Ghost is present.

On one occasion John Wesley was preaching in a downtrodden section of London. On the edge of the multitude were two ruffians. One said to the other, "Who is this preacher? We'll show him. What right has he to come here spoiling our fun?" They each reached down and took a stone in their hands. They threw back their arms ready to hurl the stones when, as the saintly preacher talked about the power of Christ to change the lives of sinful men, he seemed to be transformed with the beauty of a great light. They stood transfixed with their arms poised in the air. Then one turned to the other and said: "He ain't a man, Bill! He ain't a man!" The stones rolled away as their hearts softened. At the close of the service Wesley passed through the crowd and put his arms about their shoulders and said, "God bless you, my boys!" Whereupon one of the roughnecks said to the other: "He is a man, Bill! He is a man! He's a man like God!"

This is the question with which we are concerned. Is it possible for us to become like God? Can we deepen our spiritual lives? We answer immediately in the affirmative. It is possible. We, too, may become men and women like God. How, then, is this to come about?

Be Conscious of Sin

If we would deepen our spiritual lives, we must have a deep sense of sin. Sin! That sad, stern fact that science cannot find a hole deep enough to bury. That awful fact that education cannot teach away, and medical skill cannot cure. That hateful and abominable thing that insulted God's holy majesty, vexed his gracious Spirit, defied his power, despised his grace, trod under foot his matchless mercy, and crucified the Son of his infinite love.

The early disciples knew that there was something wrong with the world. They recognized the tremendous fact of sin. They knew their weaknesses. They were dependent upon God. They confessed their sins. Even the great apostle Paul said: "For the good that I would, I do not: but the evil which I would not, that I do" (Rom. 7:19). Peter cried: "Depart from me; for I am a sinful man" (Luke 5:8). The saintly John said: "If we say we have no sin, we deceive ourselves, and the truth is not in us" (1 John 1:8). And James said: "Confess your faults one to another, and pray one for another, that ye may be healed" (James 5:16). Christ was the remedy for sin to the disciples. No wonder they were so powerful! We need to regain a sense of sin.

St. Francis of Assisi, who tradition tells us lived so close to Christ that the nail scars appeared in his hands and feet, was once asked why he was so influential and had so much power with people. He replied: "Well, I've been thinking about that myself lately, and this is why: The Lord looked down from heaven and said, 'Where can I find the weakest, the littlest, the meanest man on the face of the earth?' Then he saw me and said, 'I've found him, and now I'll work through him. He won't be proud of it. He'll see that I am using him because of his littleness and insignificance.'" There will be no deepening of our spiritual power unless we feel as St. Francis did.

Believe Mightily in Jesus

If we would be like God, we must believe mightily in Jesus and surrender our all to him. We must believe in him with all our hearts. This is a fundamental point of Christianity. We cannot be weak at this point. We must take our stand with Jesus Christ as the Son of God, for Christianity stands or falls, lives or dies with his personality. We must believe mightily that he is God's answer to the cries of hungry humanity, and that no key ever fitted a lock better than Jesus fits a sinner's heart. He is the only Savior from sin. He is the only one of whom we can say, "Behold the Lamb of God, which taketh away the sin of the world" (John 1:29).

Those who have deep spiritual power with God believe mightily in Jesus. They obey his commandments. The early disciples were asked, "Lovest thou me more than these" (John 21:15)? They loved Jesus better than business, home, country, wealth, ease, or pleasure. Their lives expressed the spirit of that beautiful hymn by Fanny J. Crosby we love so well:

Saviour, more than life to me,
I am clinging, clinging close to Thee;
Let Thy precious blood applied,
Keep me ever, ever near Thy side.

So it must be with us if we are to grow more like him.

Surrender the Self

Jesus also says: "If any man will come after me, let him deny himself, and take up his cross daily, and follow me. For whosoever will save his life shall lose it: but whosoever will lose his life for my sake, the same shall save it" (Luke 9:23-24). The early disciples, and many others across the years, answered this call. They surrendered themselves and all that they possessed to Jesus.

An offering was once taken for foreign missions in a church in Richmond and a young man who had no money to give wrote on a slip of paper, "I have no money, but I give myself to Jesus," and put it in the plate. That man was J. Lewis Shuck, one of our first missionaries to China.

William Booth was once asked the secret of his success. He replied, "Christ has had all there is of William Booth." That great man of God, David Livingstone, who planted the kingdom of God in Africa, would not give up. He went on and on into the jungles. After successive attacks of swamp fever, his black friends built him a little hut in which to rest for a night. The next morning at four o'clock they came to find him on his knees, his head buried in his hands on the pillow. He had died in the act of prayer. A short while before, he had written in his diary, "My Jesus, my King, my Life, my All; I again dedicate my whole self to Thee." Oh, that you and I might make such a dedication of our lives to Christ! Through such consecration as this we are sure to deepen our lives spiritually.

A dear old man had a beautiful daughter by the name of Susie Parker, who became a missionary and went out to the China mainland. Before she went, friends gave her a farewell party, and they asked her father, "What do you have to say about Susie's leaving?" The old man answered, "I have nothing too precious to give to Jesus." About a year after his daughter had sailed away to China, word came that Susie had been a good missionary, but that she had been caught in a typhoid epidemic and had died. Again friends asked the old man, "What do you say now that Susie is dead?" And his reply was the same: "I have nothing too precious to give to Jesus."

Power comes to people who lay all upon the altar, surrendering all that they are and hope to be to Jesus Christ.

Bear Suffering Bravely

Personal spiritual power comes through suffering.

Marc Connelly in *Green Pastures* says, "Even being God ain't a bed of roses." God suffers. God never suffered more than when Christ died for us. We must suffer, too. Paul says, "The Spirit itself beareth witness with our spirit, that we are the children of God: and if children, then heirs; heirs of God, and joint-heirs with Christ; if so be that we suffer with him, that we may be also glorified together" (Rom. 8:16-17).

We are transformed through suffering. Suffering made George W. Truett a much greater preacher than he would otherwise have been. Troubles rightly used open within us deep resources of spiritual power. When trials are hard, there is the cross to soften them. If our troubles are rightly used, they may make us more powerful in personality and in spirituality. A minister whose little girl was killed by an automobile said with tears in his eyes, "I am a better preacher because of this great tragedy."

There was a wonderful man in our church who was a conductor on the Southern Railroad. One day as his train from Atlanta was entering Greenville, South Carolina, he was knocked off under another train and one of his legs was crushed. It took months of agony for him to learn to use an artificial limb, but after his settlement with the railroad he gave enough money to the church to provide chimes for the tower. With God's help, that man was able to bring music out of pain, chimes out of suffering. Pain can bring power.

Perhaps you have cried out of the depths of agony, "I again consecrate myself to Thee. Make me sweeter and purer." Those who know Christ can say, as did Sarah Adams:

Nearer, my God, to Thee,
Nearer to Thee!

E'en though it be a cross
That raiseth me;
Still all my song shall be,
Nearer, my God, to Thee.

Pray Without Ceasing

If we would grow in Godlikeness and spirituality, we must spend much time in prayer. Waiting hours are not wasted hours. The most profitable time we ever spend is that which we spend on our knees. Men of power are men who have been on their knees. It is said that when Kagawa, that great Japanese who was acclaimed to be the greatest Christian in the world, was once asked the secret of his wonderful life, he replied with one word: "Prayer." And we are told that Martin Luther, father of the Reformation, said that he was such a busy person that he had to pray at least four hours a day.

Prayer changes things. If Abraham prayed and God spared Lot; if Moses prayed and God sent manna from heaven and brought water out of a dry rock; if Jacob prayed and became a prince in Israel; if Joseph prayed and received a throne in Egypt; if Joshua prayed his way into the Promised Land; if Elisha prayed and it did not rain for three and a half years and then he prayed again and it rained; if Elijah prayed and God spared the widow's son; if Isaiah's prayers stayed Judah's downfall; if Daniel prayed and God closed the mouths of hungry lions; if the three Hebrew children prayed their way through the fiery furnace; if Jonah prayed and God spared Nineveh; if Hannah prayed Israel's greatest judge into existence; if Hezekiah prayed and God added fifteen years to his life; if Solomon prayed and became one of the wisest men who ever lived; if Peter prayed and became a rock; if John prayed and saw the windows of heaven open; if a dying thief prayed his way into Paradise; if Stephen prayed and saw the Son of God standing at the right hand of the throne; if the disciples prayed and Pentecost came and three thousand souls were saved; if Paul and Silas prayed their way out of prison; if a little group of women prayed Peter out of jail; and if our Lord and Savior Jesus Christ thought that prayer was so important that he often spent all night in prayer; then, my friends, there is power in prayer. And the more we pray the more we become like him, and the more of his power we share.

When Dr. Gambrell visited John Knox's church in Scotland and the janitor told him where John Knox, whose prayers the Queen of England was said to fear more than invading armies, had kneeled to pray, he exclaimed: "Stand aside, man. Let me kneel where John Knox knelt!"

All of us may not be able to kneel where the mighty John Knox knelt, but each of us should have a private place of prayer where we, too, can talk to God. We can live in such close personal communion with God that life will be for us one long, beautiful prayer. We must travel the avenue of prayer to Godlikeness.

Render Christian Service

Many are the pathways that lead to power, but there is nothing that fans the flames of spirituality and deepens us religiously like winning others to Christ. What a tragedy it is that any person could ever say at any time in history, "No man careth for my soul." Surely God's Word is right: "He that winneth souls is wise" (Prov. 11:30). When a Christian brings another to Christ, the fires of Pentecost burn within his soul.

How I love to go to Ridgecrest! I almost cut my teeth there as a boy. This great religious assembly made a profound impression on my life. One of the weeks I love best is Foreign Mission Week, when God's noble missionaries come from around the world. One summer I heard a missionary say that the past, the present, and the future of Christianity may be summed up in one word — the word "share." How true that is! What

Christ has done for us is simply too wonderful for us not to share with others.

There are many who are not sharing Christ with others as they should. My father-in-law and one of God's noblest preachers, Dr. L. M. Latimer, used to tell of a little boy whose Sunday School teacher said to him, "Son, you're lost." The boy replied, "How can I be lost?" "You are lost," said the good teacher, "if you have not accepted Christ as your Savior." The little fellow said, "I don't believe it. My mother and father go to church every time the doors are opened, and they have never told me I'm lost. I won't believe it until they tell me it's so."

What a pity! Many fathers and mothers have never attempted to win their own flesh and blood to Christ. What a superlative privilege it is for a parent to have the overwhelming joy of sharing his knowledge and experience of Christ with his or her own child.

John A. Broadus, one of the early presidents of our theological seminary in Louisville, grew up in a little country church. One day he gave his heart to Christ. One of his first thoughts was of his red-headed, freckle-faced friend named Sandy Jones. He went to Sandy and said, "Sandy, I've accepted Jesus as my Savior. Won't you accept him, too?" Sandy said, "Well, maybe I will, and maybe I won't. I just don't know."

But the next day during the revival Sandy Jones walked the aisle, and put his hand in the hand of the preacher and professed his faith in Christ. Then he went to his friend, stuck out his hand, and said, "Thank you, John, for telling me about Jesus."

When John A. Broadus was dying, he said to his wife: "Do you know what I think is going to be one of the sweetest experiences I'll have when I cross the Jordan? I think it's going to be when old Sandy Jones comes and sticks out his great big hand and says, 'Thank you, John, for telling me about Jesus.' "

Thank God we can tell people about Jesus! Thank God that

we have a Savior who was willing to die for our sins, so that if we are conscious of our failings and believe mightily in him; if we surrender ourselves and bear suffering bravely; if we pray without ceasing and serve him by serving others, we will have traveled these paths which lead to greater Christlikeness, and to power with God and with people.

3. The Indispensable Christ

JOHN 15:1-10

"Without me ye can do nothing" (v. 5).

There are many things that you and I need. There are equally as many that we can do without. But there is one thing that all of us must have, and that is Jesus Christ.

Jesus Christ makes this claim for himself in John 15:5: "Without me ye can do nothing." This is a true claim. We need not limit it by so much as a hair's breadth. History substantiates it; human experience validates it. Jesus looked the world in the face and said, "You cannot get along without me." Elsewhere he said, "I and the Father are one." So when he spoke the words of this text, it was the equivalent of saying, "You cannot get along without God."

Let us look at the claims of Jesus to be "the indispensable Christ."

Knowledge of God

He is indispensable to a true conception of God. No man is much of a theologian who does not know the God of Jesus Christ. If you were to say to me, "Paint me a picture of God," I would paint you a picture of Jesus Christ. For Jesus is God. Jesus is the perfect revelation of what God is and what man, through him, may become. No man really knows God separated from Jesus Christ. Apart from Jesus men know God by starlight; through Jesus they know God by sunlight. Jesus presents the world with a heavenly Father it may worship with the deepest of joy and serve with the greatest of adoration — one in whom is blended holiness, majesty, love, and power.

One day a mother saw her little son painting a picture and asked, "What are you painting?" The little fellow replied, "Why, Mother, I'm painting a picture of God." The mother said: "Darling, don't you know you can't do that? Nobody has ever seen God." The child replied, "When I get through they will have, because I'm painting a God like Jesus Christ."

Jesus came into this world to present God to us.

Understanding of Life

Jesus is indispensable to a satisfactory interpretation of life. No man is much of a philosopher who does not know that Jesus Christ is God's answer to every need of the human heart. Apart from Jesus men live in darkness. Separated from Jesus life is artificial, superficial. It is as the animal life of the field. Apart from Jesus Christ life is dwarfed, infinitesimal, a mere existence.

I was pastor for eleven years in a lovely little county seat town in South Carolina. I had a friend there who ran a whiskey store. Almost every day when I went to town I'd run into this friend and ask him, "How're you feeling today?" Invariably he would answer, "Oh, I'm just existing, just existing."

One day when he gave me that answer, I said to him: "Well, my friend, if you would give your heart to Jesus Christ, you wouldn't have to say 'I'm just existing.' You could say, 'I'm living, gloriously and abundantly!' " And he said: "Yes, I know that what you say is true. My mother was a Christian. But I've got to have money." And he turned quietly and walked away.

Some years later I returned to this little town and I ran into my liquor-store friend. When I put out my hand and asked how he was, tears welled up in his eyes as he said, "If I had done what you wanted me to do, I wouldn't be in the awful mess I'm in now." Then he turned and walked away toward his liquor store. And I thought of the rich young ruler who went away sorrowful.

Then one day I read in that small-town paper that my friend had died. To think that all he had ever done was just exist! That is all any person can do who does not know Christ as his Savior, for without Jesus life is but an existence. Why is it that men love darkness more than they love the light? Satan more than Christ? sin more than the Savior? Why is it that they will sell their souls for the almighty dollar?

One night my wife and I were called to go to the bedside of a beautiful young woman who lived in an expensive apartment. She had been drinking for three days and had nobody to feed her. While my wife cleaned out the empty beer cans from the kitchen to prepare food for her, I sat by her bedside and listened to her tragic story. When she had finished, I said to her, "If you only could let Jesus come into your life, life would be as beautiful for you as it should be."

No person *really* lives, separated from Jesus. Jesus solves every problem of the heart. He uncrooks every question mark. The non-Christian world groans and travails under the problem of an unintelligible universe, but Jesus and Jesus Christ alone makes this world intelligible. No person really lives, separated from Jesus.

Love for Fellowman

Next, Christ is indispensable to an adequate relationship one to another.

We are living in a world torn and divided, man against man. There is hatred, ill will, violence, and disturbance on every hand.

In the United Nations Building in New York City there is a little prayer room where a mysterious blue light glows from the marble altar. The altar was given by the country of Sweden to the United Nations and reminds all who enter of him who is the light of the world. Posted there are the flags and the names of the countries whose soldiers have given their lives in all of the wars involving member nations. Across the way on the wall is this verse from Isaiah 2:4: "They shall beat their swords into plowshares, and their spears into pruninghooks: nation shall not lift up sword against nation, neither shall they learn war any more." But such a day will never come until people everywhere know Jesus Christ as Lord and Savior, bow on their knees to him who is the Prince of Peace, and let him rule in their hearts and in the destiny of nations.

Jesus came into this world to teach men how to live together, how to love one another. Jesus teaches us that the greatest commandment of all is to "love the Lord thy God with all thy heart, and with all thy soul, and with all thy mind" (Matt. 22:37). He said the second greatest commandment is to "love thy neighbour as thyself" (v. 39). Then Jesus goes on to say, "Love your enemies." Isn't it a remarkable religion that teaches us to be good to our enemies, not to heap coals of fire upon their heads, to pray for them and not to despise them?

In *Stand by for China,* Gordon Poteat tells of a crippled girl named Miss Stewart who was a missionary to China. One day an aristocratic, educated woman of China saw Miss Stewart go hobbling up the stairway. She commented, "I didn't know Miss Stewart was crippled. How did that happen?" Her listeners then told how when Miss Stewart was a tiny baby, her parents were missionaries in China. During the Boxer Rebellion the Chinese came and murdered her mother and father, and threw her tiny body down on a concrete floor. Some bones were broken, and someone picked her up and carried her to the hospital. Later on she went to the States and was educated in a religious school. There she decided to go back to China to be a missionary. "I want to go back to the very spot on which the Chinese killed my mother and dad, and I want to tell them about Jesus," she said.

When they had finished telling her the story, the aristocratic Chinese lady said, "I want to know more about a religion like that."

Jesus Christ came to bring us such a religion. Christianity is never more beautiful than when Jesus Christ, on the cross, looks down upon his enemies who have helped to place him there, and prays, "Father, forgive them; for they know not what they do."

Oh, the magnanimity of Jesus!

Endurance of Trials

Jesus Christ is indispensable in the overwhelming crises of life. We sing the words of Annie S. Hawks:

I need Thee every hour,
Most gracious Lord;
No tender voice like Thine
Can peace afford.

We do need him every hour, but there isn't even a *second* that we can afford to be without Jesus.

If we ever needed him, how we do need him in the hour of sorrow, trial, and tragedy. As a pastor, I could give endless examples of how people have triumphed over tragedy with the help of Jesus Christ.

I think of a preacher whose wife has been in our state mental hospital for eight years, and whose son joined his mother there some time ago. This dear, aging man of God said to me, "Were it not for the grace of God, I could not bear it!"

I think about one of my deacons who called me one Christmas Eve to tell me that his family was on the way for a holiday visit, and his wife lay in the bathroom in a pool of blood, having taken her own life. They could not have faced that situation together without the help of Jesus.

I think about that disastrous fire in a large hotel in Atlanta in which 120 people were killed. As I viewed the bodies at the morgue, I wondered, How could we bear this if it were not for Jesus Christ?

I think of the morning when the news came from Paris that 105 of the finest citizens of our city had died in a plane disaster there. As I faced some of these families and tried to console them, I asked, "What comfort can they find unless they find comfort in Jesus?"

I think about how my phone rang one day and a great and distinguished lawyer from a lovely town in South Carolina said: "Our boy has been wounded in Korea. You baptized him when he was nine years old and he gave his heart to Christ. He loved you and still loves you, and we want you to know about it and to pray for him and write to him." I said I would and I did, and just a few weeks later a phone call came saying that the boy was dead. When I looked into the face of that poor, brokenhearted mother and dad at the funeral, I said, "What do parents do when they give up their only child unless they know Jesus Christ?" Only Christ can comfort. Only Christ can heal. Only Christ can save. His grace alone is sufficient. Every preacher knows what sorrow means, and knows that he cannot wend his way to the home where there is tragedy unless Jesus goes with him. No words but his words are of any avail.

Victory over Sin

Finally, Christ is indispensable — absolutely indispensable — to victory over sin. Sin — that stern, tragic fact which has cursed, blighted, wrecked, and marred this whole world in which we live — is man's worst enemy. Sin is a force that drags man downward.

Most people are careful when they are in high places. They do not run carelessly to the brink of a cliff, lest something cause them to fall. A short time ago a man and his wife and their son came to Atlanta to visit Stone Mountain, one of the most imposing pieces of exposed rock in the world. It is called Gibraltar's big brother. Thrilled to be there, the boy hurriedly climbed to the top. At the peak was an old, dilapidated fence with a sign which read: "Danger. Do not proceed beyond this point." In his excitement the boy ignored the sign. When they found his body at the foot of the mountain, they could see where his fingernails had been torn off trying to catch hold as he tumbled down. The soles of his shoes were nearly worn through with his trying to gain a foothold on the side.

Sin is like that. It drags people down like the force of gravitation; but there is a power far greater than Satan's, and that is the power of God through Jesus Christ. In every heart where Christ reigns, sin is being done to death. In the battle between the Lamb and the beast, there is full assurance for final victory for the Lamb of God "who taketh away the sin of the world."

Tom Bingham was a man who had accidentally shot out both eyes in his youth. He became a magazine salesman and eventually founded the Lighthouse for the Blind in Atlanta. But Tom, a fellow member of the Lions Club, had many problems, and some of them he shared with me.

One day his wife, a very lovely girl from Virginia, telephoned to say that Tom was in the hospital with cancer and wouldn't live. She was distraught and said to me, "I want you to do me a favor. I love Tom so much that I cannot give him up unless I know he is a Christian. If I could just know that he trusts Jesus as his Savior, I could give him up. Will you go over and speak to him?"

I said I would and when I asked him whether he had trusted Jesus, he said, "Certainly I trust in Jesus. What can a dying blind man trust in *except* Jesus Christ? He is the only Savior, Jim!"

Yes, indeed, he is! We cannot do without him. Christ is a glorious Savior who saves unto the uttermost all who trust in him.

We are told that many years ago on a wall in Cincinnati hung a painting of a chess game in which there were two participants

— one, a fine young man who moved the white pieces, the other the devil, who moved the black. The issue of the game was the young man's soul. If he won, he would be free of the devil forever. If he lost, he would be the devil's slave forever. Evidently the artist believed in the supreme power of evil over good because he entitled his picture, "The Devil Wins."

One day a great chess player stood before the painting, studying it for a long time. He wrote to an ex-chess champion in New Orleans and invited him to come to Cincinnati. As this man stood before the painting and studied it carefully, he said, "I believe there is a move this young man can take whereby he can win over the devil. Young man, take that move, take that move!"

God Almighty in his infinite wisdom and love has worked out a move that every man, woman, boy, and girl in the whole world may take from darkness to light, from danger to safety, from sin to salvation. Man, woman, boy, girl, take that move! Giving him your heart, your life, your soul, your all is the only way. Jesus is the way. We can do without everything else and anything else, but we cannot do without Jesus.

What the hand is to the lute,
What the breath is to the flute,
What is fragrance to the smell,
What the spring is to the well,
What the flower to the bee,
That is Jesus Christ to me.

What the mother to the child,
What the guide in pathless wild,
What is oil to troubled wave,
What is ransom to the slave,
What is water to the sea,
That is Jesus Christ to me.

4. Winsome Witnesses

ACTS 1:8

"Ye shall be witnesses unto me" (v. 8).

Some of us have never been in a courtroom, much less sat in the witness chair near the judge's bench. Nevertheless, we are witnesses. We are witnesses in the perennially open courtroom of Jesus Christ.

Jesus Christ is on trial today. Countless thousands of people are saying, "Give us Barabbas! Let Jesus be crucified!" As witnesses: we should be more than spectators at his trial; we should be testimony-bearers. As witnesses we should testify for the truth, though we be crushed for testifying. What we need to do is move out of the spectators' gallery into the witness box for Jesus Christ.

It is interesting that in the original language the word for witness is *martus,* from which we get our word martyr. Witnesses are martyrs in the courtroom of Jesus. They are willing to suffer that Christ may reign in the midst of the present world crisis. His witnesses are winsome witnesses.

Winsome Witnesses

In Luke 24:48 Jesus says, "Ye are witnesses of these things." There can be no such thing as a nonwitnessing Christian. How can a person not tell the story of Jesus Christ? It seems that if we hold our peace, the very stones cry out against us. Christianity is a progressive, propagative religion; it is a going religion and a growing religion. It is impossible to keep a genuine Christian from relating his miraculous experience with

Christ. For one thing, it is simply too good not to be told! What has happened to us is too marvelous, too wonderful. We must tell it or burst at the seams. We tell it spontaneously. We tell it or die. It is just too good to keep.

Too, when we consider the danger and the doom of the sinner, it is only logical that we should burst every barrier in order to tell others about Jesus Christ. Oh, the tragedy of silence!

I read recently of a young man who was riding a tractor that overturned and pinned him underneath. All who came by were anxious to lift the tractor off of him. Certainly, my friends, when we see anybody in danger of their lives, we want to rescue them. Should we not likewise want to rescue that person who is lost in sin and away from Christ?

Besides, we are under command to tell others about Jesus. Jesus Christ, the great commander-in-chief of the Christian army, says, "Go, tell." "Go ye . . . and teach." "Go thou and preach." "Go and do." "Go home to thy friends and tell them how great things the Lord hath done for thee."

Christ's word to the impenitent sinner is "Woe, and I heard an angel crying to the inhabitants of the earth, Woe, Woe." Christ's word to the penitent sinner is "Ho, come ye to the waters and drink." Christ's word to the redeemed sinner is "Go, go ye therefore, and teach all nations, baptizing them in the name of the Father, and of the Son, and of the Holy Ghost."

Those who testify for Jesus are supremely attractive. "How beautiful upon the mountains are the feet of them that bringeth good tidings." We think of Peter at Pentecost, and of Peter and John at the gate Beautiful, and of how the people "took knowledge of them that they had been with Jesus." We think of the great apostle Paul before Agrippa or Felix, and of Paul's fundamental thesis when he said, "I am not ashamed of the gospel of Christ: for it is the power of God unto salvation to every one that believeth; to the Jew first, and also to the Greek" (Rom. 1:16).

I have just returned from a preaching mission for the United

States Air Force to Germany. While there I visited both East and West Berlin and saw one of the chambers where Hitler put some of his political prisoners to death. Again and again I was reminded of how many of those he put to death went gladly, testifying for Jesus Christ.

One summer when I was at Princeton University, Mrs. Wesberry and I had the privilege of taking Dr. Martin Niemoller, who had been a political prisoner of Hitler's during the war, and his lovely wife to New York. We were in the car about two hours with them, and we shall never forget the experience. I asked Dr. Niemoller, "Why didn't Hitler kill you?" His wife answered: "I'll tell you why. Hitler was afraid of my husband. He had an uncanny feeling about Martin." The story is told that Dr. Niemoller was put in a cell with an atheist, who was to try to argue him down, to convince him that he ought to become an atheist. It wasn't long until the atheist asked for a Bible.

We cannot but admire the young politician in one of John Galsworthy's dramas who could not keep silent when his country was guilty of injustice to a smaller nation. His best friends begged him not to sacrifice his career by protesting to his superiors. His wife even left him when he made his unpopular protest. As a consequence, he had to surrender his office and was finally killed by an infuriated mob because he would not keep silent when he felt he must speak the truth.

Christ's witnesses must always speak out for him, no matter what the consequences. How beautiful such witnesses are—how winsome! The immortal Gladstone was awakened one night by a woman from the slums of London who asked him to visit her dying son. Gladstone got up and made his way into the slums and climbed the attic stairs and sat down by the little fellow. He planted a kiss on his brow, gave him a gift, and told the lad about Jesus. The next day as he went to Parliament, someone said to him, "Mr. Gladstone, we hope you have a great message for Parliament today." Mr. Gladstone is reported to have said: "I do not know whether I have a great message for Parliament or not, but one thing I know: there is not a happier man in all of England." The happiest, most attractive, most radiant people in the world are those who witness for Jesus Christ.

What a difference it makes if we break our cowardly silences. We do not need more preachers today; we need better preachers. If preaching could save us, our nation would have been saved a long time ago. What we need is more of the real religion of Jesus Christ. His religion lives, not only in the pulpit and in the pews on Sundays, but in our daily lives.

The public is astonishingly ignorant of the Bible. People are not studying the Bible. But they *are* reading the lives of professing Christians. How inarticulate are the lives of many! How we do need to fit the description that Tolstoy made of Lincoln when he said, "He was a miniature Christ." Or, as was said of Isaac Watts, we too should be "a bit of Christ." We are daily editions of the gospel of Jesus Christ. Someone has put it:

> You are writing a Gospel,
>   A chapter a day,
> In deeds that you do,
>   And in words that you say.
>
> Men read what you write,
>   Whether false or true.
> Say, what is the Gospel
>   According to you?

Witnessing Witnesses

Jesus' witnesses are not only winsome; they are also active, *witnessing* witnesses.

Of what? you ask. Jesus said, "Ye are my witnesses." Of what are we to testify?

There was once an aged saint of God who in her earlier life had memorized many passages of Scripture. But in the last weeks of her life her memory weakened, and she could not recall but one verse. She repeated that verse over and over: "I know whom I have believed, and am persuaded that he is able to keep that which I have committed unto him against that day" (2 Tim. 1:12). As her condition grew worse and the gates of heaven opened wider and wider, she could not repeat all of the verse, but she was heard to say, "I know him." Then in the last moments of her life when her eyes were closing, in a faint whisper she was heard to say, "Him, Him, Him." That, my friends, is the witness that we ought to bear.

We find a beautiful illustration of this in the book of Genesis. Abraham wished to find a bride for his son Isaac. He commissioned Eliezer to go to Mesopotamia to look for a bride. At a well in the city of Nahor, Eliezer met Rebecca. Of what did he speak? He didn't talk about himself. He talked about Isaac, his master. He probably spoke of his hair, the color of his eyes, the shape of his mouth, his hands, and his feet. He talked about his personality. He made Isaac so attractive that Rebecca had to say yes.

Jesus is the bridegroom. The church is his bride. You and I are to lead and win people to the bride for the bridegroom. Our witness must ever be of him who is altogether lovely.

Worldwide Witnesses

Now, what are these things of which we are witnesses?

Jesus told his disciples that they had witnessed the fulfilment of all those prophecies "which were written in the law of Moses, and in the prophets, and in the psalms concerning me" (Luke 24:44). There it was written that he would suffer and die and rise from the dead the third day, and "that repentance and remission of sins should be preached in his name to all nations, beginning from Jerusalem" (v. 47).

Jesus' disciples are not only to be witnessing witnesses; they are to be *world* witnesses. Theirs is an all-sufficient message, a comprehensive message — one that includes town missions, city missions, county missions, state missions, home missions, Convention-wide, nationwide, and worldwide missions. Ours is a witness of the suffering and resurrected Christ, of the necessity of repentance, and of the possibility of forgiveness. It covers the whole wide world.

These verses spoken by Jesus come at the close of what Ernest Renan has called the most beautiful book in the world, the longest of the four Gospels. Luke's purpose in writing this Gospel to the most excellent Theophilus, a cultured Greek, was to tell the works, life, and teachings of Jesus in such a convincing manner that Theophilus might know beyond a shadow of a doubt that Christianity is the one true religion. That is the witness that we are to take to the whole wide world.

From Greenland's icy mountains,
From India's coral strand;
Where Africa's sunny fountains
Roll down their golden sand;
From many an ancient river,
From many a palmy plain,
They call us to deliver
Their land from error's chain.

Rosalee Mills Appleby has written a beautiful book which has influenced and changed the lives of many persons. It is entitled *The Life Beautiful.* In her book Mrs. Appleby tells us that a beautiful life is an outflowing life. She says:

> If Christ is the door, you are the doorkeeper, to open or close it for others. If he is the light of the world, you are the bearer of that light to the end of the earth. If he is the vine, you are the fruit-bearing branch that draws life from that vine. If he is the bread of life, you are to break it to feed those who hunger. If he is the truth, you are the truth-bearer, the interpretation of the truth. If he is the bright and morning star, you are to brush aside the clouds that veil his beauty from the world, that humanity may see and live forever. Oh, glorious truth that we are an indispensable part of the great plan and program of the Father!

Winning Witnesses

Jesus Christ's witnesses are winsome. They are actively witnessing. They are witnesses to the world. They are winning witnesses. Jesus Christ has assured his witnesses that they can win: "Ye shall receive power, when the Holy Spirit is come upon you." His witnesses cannot fail because he is with them. They will not be mechanical, materialistic, or professional witnesses; they will be supernatural witnesses.

After Jesus' great commission to his disciples, he said, "Lo, I am with you alway, even unto the end of the world." He also added, "Tarry ye in the city until ye be clothed with power from on high." Here, my friends, is the secret of spiritual success. Have you been wondering why your witness is so ineffective? What sort of clothing do you wear? Have you been wrapped in divine clothing?

A man's clothing may be his most predominant characteristic. Aristophanes was clothed with audacity, Plutarch with nobility; but the Christian's outstanding characteristic is power. This is the garment that God gives.

The word "power" comes from the same word from which we get our word dynamite. You say, "Why, that's an explosive!" Yes, it is an explosive. Dynamite is revolutionary; it changes things. It is powerful, and that is exactly what the Christian religion is. Jesus' witnesses must change the world.

I shall never forget perhaps the most important lesson I learned in the ministry. I was a student at Mercer University when I went to hold my first revival. I took a bus from Macon down to Bainbridge, Georgia, to a large country church. I had worked hard all summer to prepare about eight sermons. I had them all written out in a little black book. It was a long, long ride, and as I traveled along in the bus, I remembered that there was a judge in this community. I began to think of the schoolteachers who would probably be at the meeting. As I thought about the fact that I was only a sophomore in college, I wondered, What do I know compared to these people? Many of them had been Christians longer than I. I had never preached in a revival. What did I know about it? I found myself frightened to death.

Then in the midst of my fear, when I was about to wish that I might turn around and go home, someone got on the bus and came and sat by my side. He said, "Son, you're worried. What's troubling you?" I said: "I'm going to hold a revival meeting, and I've never held one before. I'm scared. I don't think I can do it." He said, "Don't you remember that when I called you to preach, I said, 'And lo, I am with you alway, even unto the end of the world'?" And it dawned on me what Christ's promise meant. I went on and held that revival, trusting in Jesus to stand by me, and trusting in the Holy Spirit to inspire me. I give you my word of honor that I have never had a greater revival than on that occasion. God did some strange and wonderful things. I had learned that the secret of success in witnessing is to turn everything over to Jesus Christ, and to let the Holy Spirit have his way in our lives.

When David Livingstone went back to Glasgow and addressed the university there, the students had assembled in a spirit of ridicule. But as they gazed upon his face, blackened by the African sun, and at his lion-injured arm limp by his side, they grew quiet. At the conclusion one of them rose and asked, "Dr. Livingstone, what was it that enabled you to keep on out there in Africa?" He replied: "If you would know what it was that sustained me in my loneliness, gave me strength when I could not bear the food which was offered me, was my help among those whose language I could not speak, and gave endurance for all the unspeakable trials which beset me, I will tell you. It was the promise of Jesus to his church: 'Go . . . and, lo, I am with you alway.' "

The omnipresent spirit of God is available for all who would have power to carry out their mission in life. There can be no

Christlikeness without Christ-inbreathing. Such anointment is not substitutional but supplementary.

The great English painter Herkomer's father lived with him at Bushy. The father had once been successful in modeling clay, but in his old age he had lost his ability and was sorrowful. His son knew this, and while his father slept, he went into the studio, took the tools, and made his father's feeble attempt as beautiful as art could make it. When the old man awakened in the morning and looked upon his work, he exclaimed: "Ah, I can do it as well as I ever did! See? The work speaks for itself!" It is in just such a way as this that the Spirit of God comes and supplements our feeble efforts, correcting our blunders and imperfections, and makes us effective witnesses.

Hurrying out of an art gallery, a young man passed by an old man standing by a magnificent painting of Jesus. The sight caught his eye, and the young man turned and tarried to look up at the painting of Jesus. He said to the old man, "That's a magnificent painting." "It certainly is," the gentleman replied, "and it has a good name, sir. It's called 'The Man of Galilee.' " The young man turned and left, and the old man went away. But on his way, the young man decided he would return to the gallery. As he stood at the foot of that painting of Jesus, he looked up into the eyes of the Man of Galilee and said, "Oh, Man of Galilee, if there's anything I can do for you, you can count on me."

There *is* something that we can do for him. Jesus said, "Ye shall be my witnesses." We can all witness for Christ. We can move out of the spectators' gallery and into the witness box for Jesus Christ.

5. Opening Heaven's Gates

MARK 1:14-15

"Repent ye, and believe the gospel" (v. 15).

Jesus' first public message was a challenge to repentance. Repentance is the keynote of his entire ministry, the chief characteristic of all his preaching, the demand he made on all those who would become followers of him.

"Now after that John was put in prison, Jesus came into Galilee, preaching" (v. 14). *Jesus came preaching!* And my, what a preacher he was! He came proclaiming, publishing, declaring, crying out, speaking, talking. He was sure of his message; he knew what to preach. He had a tremendous manifesto, and he delivered it with authority and power. "All authority was given unto him in heaven and in earth." He was history's supreme dogmatist on God's love and righteousness and on man's sin and selfishness. He was sure of his ground; he knew contradiction. He was not concerned about the criticism of man. He was neither dry nor dull. He was not an intellectual apologist. He was a dynamic and thrilling preacher of the gospel message, and he went to the very essence of things.

Some years ago a minister said that we ought to declare a moratorium on preaching. This was not Jesus. Jesus teaches us in his parable of the soils that nothing will ever take the place of preaching. The kingdom of God will come in large measure because of the preached message. We learn by his example and teaching that preaching is the best method of promoting the kingdom of God.

The Time Is Now

Jesus said, "The time is fulfilled." The fulness of time has arrived — the time that all ages have looked forward to is here and now.

"The kingdom of God is at hand." He who said, "Seek ye first the kingdom of God," put the kingdom of God first in his own life. He gave the kingdom priority, the implicit kingdom of God that lies beneath the ruins of this world, the real world which we could never fully find ourselves. He came revealing the world of God. He came telling men of their real selves that lie dormant within them. He came telling them the good news that men do not have to be enslaved and held as prisoners by the prince of this world. He came to open the eyes of the human race that were blinded by conceit. He came to release an imprisoned world made captive by its own folly.

This, my friends, was extraordinary good news! It was news of the reign and rule of God in the hearts of men; news of the reign of God's love, righteousness, and peace; news of the supremacy of light, truth, and love. Paul said, "The kingdom of God is not meat and drink; but righteousness, and peace, and joy in the Holy Ghost (Rom. 14:17). He came preaching the kingdom of God — not a national political institution, but the spiritual reign of God in the actual life of men. He came to say that God is the King and the Father, and that we are subject to his rule. As he is our heavenly Father, we are his family, and he is the overseer of his family.

Jesus speaks of two worlds in deadly conflict with each other: God's world and the world of evil. He tells us that God wants to break through the world of evil. He wants something to happen to man. "A great possibility wants to become actual in man's impossibility. A great emancipation wants to eventuate in man's imprisonment. A great affirmation wants to devour man's doubt. A great transcendence wants to make a lie of man's limiting existence. A great miracle wants to deny law. A great life wants forever to swallow up man's death. An Easter wants to shatter our Calvary-tombs!" God wants to break in upon man's dark world. No time must be wasted. Seek ye the kingdom of God; knock, enter, and pray.

The Message is Repent!

"Repent ye, and believe the gospel," says Jesus. Repent. This is the message that Nathan preached to David long ago. This is the message that John the Baptist came preaching in the wilderness of Judea. This is the message he preached to King Herod concerning his violation of the Seventh Commandment. John the Baptist was beheaded for preaching the gospel of repentance.

Jesus took up the message of his forerunner. The kingdom of God was promised through the Messiah, and it was at hand. One thing was left for man to do, and that was to break with his sins, to enter into the kingdom, and to believe and have confidence in God's good news.

Two things are essential for entrance into the kingdom of God: one is repentance, the other is faith. Repentance and faith are as inseparable as Siamese twins. They are like two spokes in the same wheel, like two hinges on a door. We must walk by faith and not by sight, and in the eye there must be the tear of repentance. If there is no faith, there is no repentance; if there is no repentance, there is no faith. One cannot be a true believer without penitence.

What did Jesus mean when he said, "Repent"? Literally, the word repent means to change your mind. The story is told of a boy who one day brought a geometry problem to Dr. Temple, the headmaster at Rugby. The boy had made a hopeless muddle of the problem, and Dr. Temple said, "My boy, you must think." "I did think, sir," the lad replied. "Well, think again, and think differently," said the headmaster. This, my friends, is what real repentance is. It is thinking again and thinking differently.

"Repent" is a beautiful word, but it has been corrupted, altered, misinterpreted, and misunderstood. There have been many substitutes for it. There are some who think they have repented and they have not. The word means to change your mind, to be sorry enough for your sins that you are willing to quit them.

Paul tells us there are two kinds of sorrow for sins: there is godly sorrow and worldly sorrow. "Godly sorrow worketh repentance to salvation not to be repented of: but the sorrow of the world worketh death" (2 Cor. 7:10).

Worldly sorrow is a superficial sort of sorrow; it touches only the surface. Its thought rises no higher than man himself. He is sorry because he is afraid his sin will find him out. He is sorry because he has to be punished for his sins. A man sins, and his conscience hurts him, and he says: "I wish I had not done that; I have been foolish." But the next time he is tempted, he yields again, and soon it is easy to yield. He feels less and less sorrow as time goes on. Sin becomes easier and easier, his conscience duller and duller, and the feeling of wrong dies out.

When men go to prison, they say, "I'm sorry I was caught." Satan himself is perhaps sorry for sin, and ashamed of being the devil, and may be so throughout all eternity, but he never really repents.

Real repentance is in knowing pain, in feeling a sense of guilt. It is the most miserable of all feelings. It makes a man hate himself, feel at war with himself and with God. Such a terrible feeling as this can lead man to death. He says, "I am bad. I hate myself. God hates me. All I can do is try to forget my unhappiness." Soul suicide is an awful tragedy.

Judas is an eminent example of worldly sorrow. His sorrow did not save him; it drove him to despair. He had deep remorse, and went out and committed suicide. If he had begged for forgiveness and expressed real sorrow, he would have been forgiven and been restored.

Peter repented. He went out and wept bitterly, and he had godly sorrow and was forgiven and restored.

There are other paltry substitutes for repentance. One of them is extravagant emotionalism. The hell-fire evangelist comes and preaches, and the people are stirred. They are moved to tears. Sometimes there are those who break down and sob. They think they have repented, but within a few weeks that shallow emotionalism wears off.

True repentance is far more than a matter of tears or sleepless nights, of being worried or troubled or merely convicted of sin. These feelings are fine; we ought to weep over our sins. We ought to be sorry for our sins and afraid of them. But this alone is not enough. We must be more than emotionally stirred.

There is another type of repentance which might be called sickbed repentance. When a person thinks he is going to die, he gets very religious. He asks God to let him get well, and promises that if he gets well, he'll do great things for God. Then when he does get well, he forgets the promises he has made. He is as pious as the pope when he is sick, but as devilish as a demon when well.

Sickbed repentance is not real repentance, though illness sometimes leads to real repentance. A man may be brought to know God or to have godly sorrow over his sins because of his sickness, or some sorrow or trouble that has come into his life.

Another substitute for repentance is sacrifice. The ancient Jews thought that the repentance God required was burnt offerings and sacrifices, and that if they could only offer enough bullocks on God's altar, he would forgive them. But they found that they were mistaken. What God requires is a contrite and a broken heart. He requires righteousness. He says, "Bring no more vain oblations; . . . cease to do evil; learn to do well; seek judgment, relieve the oppressed, judge the fatherless, plead for the widow." Then, and then only, "though your sins be as scarlet, they shall be as white as snow" (Isa. 1:13-18). And in Ezekiel 18:27 the Lord says, "When the wicked man turneth away from his wickedness that he hath committed, and doeth that which is lawful and right, he shall save his soul alive."

Ascetic sorrow is also a poor substitute for repentance. There are those who punish themselves bitterly for their sins. They enter a monastery, deny the world, and live a life of recluse, giving up all that makes life pleasant in order to atone for their sins. Many good and pious men and women have tried this kind of life and have found that making themselves miserable helps no more than offering burnt offerings. Their consciences are not relieved; they are not comforted. They say, "I have not punished myself enough; this punishment did not satisfy." So they try to torture themselves more, but the more they torture themselves, the more they find that they have not really repented. They try again, and they fail. They kill themselves piecemeal by slow torment, but they find no relief.

On the other hand, there is that which Paul refers to as godly sorrow, sorrow after the mind of God. It looks upon sin as God does; it hates sin. We who really repent must see sin through the eyes of God. We must grieve over our sins. We must be like David of old, saying, "Against thee, thee only, have I sinned, and done this evil in thy sight" (Ps. 51:4). David, of course, had sinned against others, but godly sorrow brought him to the feet of God, saying, "I have sinned against thee."

Again Peter, though he denied Christ on that last dark night, repented of his sin and went out in the darkness and wept. He became the preacher at Pentecost, a great rock. Tradition tells us that he was crucified with his head downward for Christ.

True repentance is a heart broken over sin, a change of mind, a turning from sin to God, a real desire to make restitution and to amend our lives in the future.

Repentance is to leave
    The sins we loved before;
And show that we in earnest grieve,
    By doing so no more.

When the heart is broken over sin, God will forgive. Jesus says, "Repent ye, and believe the gospel."

The Consequence Is Certain

Now we come to the saddest part of this sermon.

What about the impenitent? What about those who refuse to repent?

There is another important word from Jesus in Luke 13:2 concerning the Galileans that Pilate had slaughtered. The people asked Jesus if this happened because of their sins. He said, "I tell you, Nay: but, except ye repent, ye shall all likewise perish." He meant that the bloody slaughter would be repeated and that sinners would suffer in a similar way and perish unless they repented. It is repent or perish; repent or suffer; repent or be punished. There is no alternative.

Preaching is a tremendous responsibility; every minister has to render an account. May God forbid that I should ever say to people that sin is not punished. I do not want anyone to stand in the day of judgment and say to me: "You flattered me. You did not tell me the whole truth, the solemnities of eternity, the doom of sinners. You seemed to be afraid to speak the whole truth." What a terrible indictment this would be.

Unless you repent, you who are living in sin will all likewise perish. Unless you change your way of living, you will die in your sins and go into eternity without God. God wants to save you, to make you over, to change your life, to clothe you with his righteousness. He has done all in his power to bring you to repentance. "The goodness of God leadeth thee to repentance" (Rom. 2:4). He has left nothing undone. Christ died upon Calvary's cross, and if you go to your grave without Christ, you must go by way of the cross. If you refuse — if you are really stubborn and disobedient — then you will perish. "God is angry with the wicked every day. If he turn not, he will whet his sword; he hath bent his bow, and made it ready" (Ps. 7:11-12).

There is no man living who believes more in the goodness, love, mercy, holiness, and longsuffering of God than I do. But I must say, my friends, that I also believe that God is a God of judgment, of justice; that God is displeased with the wicked; that he will not tolerate our sins always. The time comes when he becomes angry with the wicked, and his wrath falls upon those who disobey him. I warn you that God hates your sins. As you stand in the judgment seat, if you do not repent of your sins, he will sharpen his sword against you. What happens beyond this world to those who die without Jesus Christ is worse than literal fire. As Ernest Baxter used to say: "Sinner, turn or burn; it is the only alternative. Turn or burn!"

I am not trying to frighten you. You cannot frighten people into the kingdom of God. I wouldn't try if I could because my method is one of love. Men are not frightened into goodness; they are not bullied into religion. But this is a fact of God's truth: Be sure your sins will find you out. If you sow a field of sin, you will reap a harvest of sin.

There are a number of reasons why.

One is that it is a natural law of the universe. "Whatsoever a man soweth, that shall he also reap." This is true in the physical realm; it is true in the spiritual realm. It is inevitable. There is no sin that is not punished.

Second, God cannot and will not allow sin to go unpunished. I cannot imagine God rewarding the wicked and the righteous equally. God will always do the right thing; he went even to the cross to help man. He took man's punishment upon himself, and he will bear our stripes if we will let him. But if we refuse, if we disobey and oppose God, then we must take the consequences. Punishment is natural and necessary. God will make every allowance; he will be kind and merciful to all, especially sinners, but he will deal with them with a stern hand. A good God will always do that which is right, and a good God cannot condone sin.

Third, if you do not repent you cannot be forgiven. To forgive an impenitent sinner would be to confirm him in his ways, to teach him to do evil. If God said: "You are living in sin; you love sin; you are going from bad to worse, but I forgive you," this would license iniquity. The foundations of the social order would be removed, and moral anarchy would follow. As long as God lives, there can be no promise of mercy to those who continue in their evil ways and refuse to acknowledge wrongdoing. No rebel can expect pardon for treason while he lives in open revolt. The judge of the earth will not put our sins away if we refuse to put them away ourselves.

Fourth, if you think there is no punishment for sin, read the Bible. It says, "The wages of sin is death." Did the sin of Adam and Eve go unpunished? What about Cain's sin? Noah's sin? The sins of Sodom and Gomorrah? Jonah? Jacob? Belshazzar? David? Nebuchadnezzar? Achan? Samson and Delilah? Judas? Dives? The whole Bible condemns sin, and it condemns you if you continue in your sins. As R. G. Lee has said, "Payday comes someday."

If God does not condemn sin, then we'd better rewrite some of these verses from the Bible:

"God spared not the angels that sinned, but cast them down to hell, and delivered them into chains of darkness, to be reserved unto judgment; and spared not the old world" (2 Pet. 2:4-5).

"Then will I profess unto them, I never knew you: depart from me, ye that work iniquity" (Matt. 7:23).

"These shall go away into everlasting punishment: but the righteous into life eternal" (Matt. 25:46).

"The Son of man shall send forth his angels, and they shall gather out of his kingdom all things that offend, and them which do iniquity; and shall cast them into a furnace of fire: there shall be wailing and gnashing of teeth" (Matt. 13:41-42).

"Then shall he say also unto them on the left hand, Depart from me, ye cursed, into everlasting fire, prepared for the devil and his angels" (Matt. 25:41).

"Ye serpents, ye generation of vipers, how can ye escape the damnation of hell?" (Matt. 23:33)

What is the meaning of all this? We cannot argue these words away because these are the words of the Lord Jesus. You are wrong if you say, "Sin is not punished, but conscience speaks with a loud voice and makes cowards of us all." Christ demands real repentance. He demands the kind of repentance that changes our minds and our lives, as illustrated in the life of Zacchaeus. Zacchaeus said, "Behold, Lord, the half of my goods I give to the poor; and if I have taken any thing from any man by false accusation, I restore him fourfold" (Luke 19:8).

Real repentance affects outward conduct. Real repentance is repentance in which we leave off those sins that we have committed. One leak can sink a ship. One sin can sink a soul. We cannot hold onto our sins.

Repentance must be immediate. There are those who say, I'm going to postpone, to delay, to procrastinate; I'm going to wait until I grow old, until I am on my deathbed; then I will repent. If you say this, you are deceiving yourselves. Few people ever change after a long life of sin. Death comes unawares, and men drop dead on the streets. We cannot afford to come to our deathbeds without Christ. A Jewish rabbi said: "Let every man repent one day before he dies; and since he may die tomorrow, let him take heed to turn from his evil ways today." Now is the time for repentance.

Christ demands hearty repentance. He wants the whole soul to be his and his forever.

He wants perpetual repentance. Certainly if we repent once, and exercise faith in the Lord Jesus Christ, we are saved from our sins. But we must continue to repent and perpetually abhor evil. Life becomes a matter of daily penitence. We are forever asking God to forgive us. Life is not sweeping away the dust one day, or cutting down the weeds and leaving the roots; it is uprooting sins, now and forever. We must repent every day of our lives.

One of the most beautiful poems ever written is Thomas Moore's *Romance of Lalla Rookh.* It is a poem on paradise and the Peri. The Peri were descendants of fallen angels who had been shut out of heaven until they could bring to heaven's gates the most precious thing in the world. The poem begins with one Peri weeping outside the gates of paradise, and an angel on guard, who says:

The Peri yet may be forgiven
Who brings to this Eternal Gate
The Gift that is most dear to heaven.

So the Peri travels to India and there sees a youthful warrior, dying in defense of liberty. She runs and catches the last drop of the patriot's blood and hurries with it back to heaven. The angel says:

See, alas, the crystal bar
Of Eden moves not — holier far
Than e'en this drop the boon must be,
That opes the gates of heaven for thee."

So the Peri sets out again, this time searching the mountains of Africa, and there she finds a beautiful maiden who has braved the dangers of a plague-infested region to minister to her stricken lover. She falls victim to the disease and dies by his side, and the Peri softly steals her last farewell sigh. She hurries back to heaven, thinking that nothing can be dearer than the "precious sigh of pure, self-sacrificing love." But the angel with regret says:

Peri, see, the crystal bar
Of Eden moves not — holier far

Than even this sign the boon must be,
        That opes the gates of heaven for thee.

In Syria's land of roses the Peri sees an innocent child at play. A robber rides up on his hot steed and dismounts to drink from a running stream. His features are hardened with sin and crime. Then vespers call the child to prayer, and the lad kneels down and prays. The robber sees him, and tears of repentance roll down his cheeks:

"There was a time," he said in mild,
        Heart-humble tones, "thou blessed child,
When young and happy, pure as thou,
        I looked and prayed like thee, but now —"
He hung his head — each nobler aim
        And hope and feeling, which had slept
From boyhood's hour, that instant came
        Fresh o'er him, and he wept.

The thief went and knelt beside the child, and up in heaven the angel smiled. The light of his smile fell on the tear that wet the criminal's face and the Peri flew and caught the tear as it fell, then winged her way back to heaven. The angel smiled and said, "Come in," and the Peri shouted,

Joy, joy, forever! My task is done —
        The gates are passed and heaven is won."

My friends, heaven's gates are opened by tears of repentance, and through our faith in the Lord Jesus Christ.

"The kingdom of God is at hand: repent ye, and believe the gospel."

6.
Better Than a Sheep

MATTHEW 12:12

"How much then is a man better than a sheep" (v. 12).

In Matthew 12:12 Jesus asks this quaint and interesting question in a synagogue on the sabbath: "How much then is a man better than a sheep?"

How much more valuable a sheep is than a man is depends entirely upon the kind of measuring rods employed. If value is determined by weight, there are some sheep that would outweigh some men. If value is determined by money, there are some breeds of sheep that would bring as much as ten or fifteen thousand dollars. If value is a question of wool to be made into fine blankets, certainly no man can produce wool. If value is found in contentment of mind, then of course a sheep would come out on top.

Despite all this, there are few who would not agree that a man is of more value than a sheep.

There are some values that cannot be measured on the scales. You and I have some qualities in common with sheep; we have life, for example. But life has a variety of forms. Through all of its subtle gradations — from the first tremors in the nerves of an angleworm or some low form of marine life, to the delicate vibrations of grey matter in the brain of the most brilliant of men, it is all life. But what a wide range of estimates we place upon these varied forms of life. How, then, shall we weigh life? How shall we gauge it? What are some of the standards that we should apply?

By Time?

First, shall we measure life by time — by days, weeks, months, years, or even by decades?

When the biographer of Methuselah was seeking material on his life, he apparently found nothing but these facts: Methuselah had a large family, he lived to be 969 years of age, and then he died. Is this all there is to life? Is the length of one's life its highest prize? Does he who lives longest always live best? In order to live splendidly, is it necessary to reach threescore and ten years?

Just as the size of the canvas does not necessarily determine the value of the painting, neither does the number of our years determine the true value of our lives. That great Roman statesman, Seneca, said: "It is possible, rather usual, for man who has lived long to have lived too little." This is why we say the good die young. Life, my friends, was never meant to be judged by years.

Perhaps you have heard of the traveler who journeyed to the land of perpetual sunshine. There were no changing seasons there, no sunsets, no sunrises. Consequently they never measured time. One never grew old there. If we think of life only in terms of time, we are sure to be disappointed and disillusioned.

It is true that we should ripen with the years in greater health, broader judgment, maturer wisdom, deeper sympathies, softened sorrows, more subdued passions, greater joy, and more eager anticipation. This is what life should do for us on the upgrade. But on the downgrade, when life begins to lapse into darkness and decay, it brings sadness and disillusionment; it wears us out; it robs us of the rich enthusiasm of living. It teaches us that there are some things we cannot do; it brings us at last, spent and weary, to the very gates of death itself.

I beg you, my friends, not to think of life as a mere matter of time. Measured by the calendar, life is but a second, infinitesimal. Individual life is but an imperceptible vibration in the infinite throb of cosmic life. "For a thousand years in thy sight," the Scriptures say, "are but as yesterday when it is past, and as a watch in the night" (Ps. 90:4). Life is as a flood, as a sleep, as the grass, which today is, and tomorrow is cut down and cast into the oven. Life is as a tale, a sigh, a dream, a breath of wind. Against all of this, what is man's puny life of threescore and ten years? Surely we should cry with the psalmist, "Teach us to number our days, that we may apply our hearts unto wisdom" (v. 12).

Thomas Randolph has a poem, "He Lives Long Who Lives Well," which speaks to the question of whether life is measured by time:

Wouldst thou live long? the only means are these—
'Bove Galen's diet, or Hippocrates'
Strive to live well; tread in the upright ways,
And rather count thy actions than thy days:
Then thou has lived enough amongst us here,
For every day well spent count a year.
Live well, and then, how soon soe'er thou die,
Thou art of age to claim eternity.
But he that outlives Nestor, and appears
To have passed the date of gray Methuselah's years,
If he his life to sloth and sin doth give,
I say he only was—he did not live.

By Money?

We cannot measure life, my friends, from the standpoint of time. But if we cannot, how shall we measure it? Shall we measure it from the standpoint of money? Does he who accumulates the most money get the most out of life? This is certainly one of the standards men apply to life. We say of a certain man, He's worth so much money. If you were to write the epitaph of a wealthy friend, would you say, This man got the most out of life because he accumulated the most money?

The true value of a man cannot be stated in dollars and

cents. The assessor's books do not tell us anything of a man's heart or the qualities of his mind and soul. The assessor's books are silent concerning the flavor and the strength of a man's personality. Though its banks be filled with deposits and its ships of commerce travel many seas, civilization is a dismal failure unless an appraisement of human life shall be at its apex. Oliver Goldsmith wrote:

> Ill fares the land, To hastening ills a prey,
> Where wealth accumulates, And men decay.

Are some of us really fooled into thinking that the real value of life rests upon wealth? Does financial success offer security, power, respect of our fellowmen, a chance to figure in the affairs of the world? Is wealth life's summum bonum? Is life summed up in beautiful homes, rich and costly apparel, glittering jewelry, servants, ease, and luxury? If your life is based on such an assumption, you are going to be greatly disillusioned. I would have you think seriously upon that striking cartoon drawn by Christ and placed in Luke's Gospel.

A rich farmer went out one day and looked over his crops, and saw that the land had brought forth plentifully. He said: "I know what I'm going to do. I'm going to tear down the old barns and build new ones. I'll say to my soul, eat, drink, and be merry." But as he was thinking about what a good time he was going to have, how he was going to store up his goods, how he was going to eat, drink, and live in merriment, and enjoy worldly pleasure, God spoke to his soul. God said, "This night thy soul shall be required of thee: then whose shall those things be?" (See Luke 12:16-20).

I ask you the same question: Whose shall they be? You can't take them with you. You brought nothing into the world; you can carry nothing out of the world.

Leo Tolstoy tells a story of a Russian peasant who was dissatisfied with his life until he visited a rich relative who offered him, for the price of one hundred rubles, all the land that he could cover in a day. This man was to start out early in the morning and run all day, and this he did. He ran and ran and ran, and finally at the end of the day, he fell over on his face. When they turned him over, blood gushed out of his mouth, and they felt his pulse and found that he was dead. They went out and dug a hole seven feet long and buried him in it. Tolstoy's conclusion is that all the land a man needs is seven feet.

Surely, my friends, we cannot measure life by the amount of money — or land — we have.

By Knowledge?

Then how shall we measure life? Shall we measure it by knowledge?

We are told, and on good authority, to "get wisdom, get understanding: . . . wisdom is the principal thing" (Prov. 4: 5-7). It is more to be desired than rubies, more precious than fine gold. Knowledge is the tree of life to those who lay hold of her. "All the things that may be desired are not to be compared to [wisdom]" (8:11). The world belongs to the man who knows.

When Socrates was asked the difference between an educated man and an uneducated man, he replied, "The difference between daylight and darkness." Every person should love knowledge and want an education. But in order to be valuable, knowledge must be used and used rightly. There was a man by the name of William Cullen Keppt whom tradition says a rich relative willed twenty-five hundred dollars a year, as long as he chose to remain in college. He entered college at the age of sixteen and remained until he was sixty-five. He earned thirteen degrees. But when he died, someone wrote an editorial about him and said that if he ever wrote a word or said anything or did anything that lived after he died, no one knew anything about it. Useless knowledge profits no one.

Too, knowledge may be misused or abused. I shudder to think what knowledge could do in the hands of unredeemed men. I shudder to think how the atomic bomb, hydrogenous power, or intercontinental balistic missiles might be used in the hands of educated but unregenerated humanity.

Is, then, the measure of a man's life to be found in these curious, great convolutions of the brain which make possible his intellectual life, or in the amount of knowledge he acquires by the use of his brain? If we cannot measure life from the standpoint of knowledge, then how shall we measure it?

By Success?

While a student at Mercer University, I was walking to class one morning when I saw, dangling from the roof of the Administration Building, which is six stories high, a wagon. It must have been taken apart, carried up the stairway, and then reassembled on the roof. But how it got there, no one was certain.

Rufus Weaver, that great and wonderful President, sent out word that he wanted everyone in chapel that day, and when he arrived you could have heard a pin drop. He turned to the hall crowded with students and said, "Gentlemen, my subject this morning is 'Hitch Your Wagon to a Star.' "

Suppose one does hitch his wagon to a star and climb the royal stairs to the hall of fame. Is fame everything? Does he gain the most who achieves his ambition in life? Browning wrote, "A man's reach should exceed his grasp, / Or what's a heaven for?" George Eliot said that what makes life dreary is want of motive. High motive is indispensable. The most heroic battles fought have been fought against odds. But does this accurately measure the real value of life?

We cannot say that achievement alone measures the full value of a man's life. You recall the Indian fable of the chief who commanded each of his sons to climb the mountain and bring back some object as a token of the highest point to which he'd climbed. Toward sundown the three sons returned. One had climbed halfway up the mountain and brought back a cluster of wild flowers. One had climbed two-thirds of the way and brought back a specimen of rare stones. The bravest of them all, perhaps, had gone to the top of the mountain, but he brought nothing back. He said: "Father, I have nothing to show for my labors. But from the heights which I reached, I caught sight of the sea."

Some people never catch sight of the sea. In fact, some people are like the monkey who bargained to work long and hard for the elephant in exchange for a barrelful of nuts. He did work long and hard; in fact, he worked so long and so hard that when at last it came time for him to get his barrelful of nuts, he had no teeth with which to crack them.

There are many people like that in life's mad, ambitious race. Once when I was in Dallas, I saw an article in the newspaper that said that Sam Rayburn, Speaker of the House of Representatives, had joined a little Baptist church. I had served as acting chaplain in the House for several weeks one summer, and I knew Mr. Sam quite well. So I clipped the article and wrote him a note, telling him how glad I was to see that he'd accepted Christ and joined the church. A few days later I received a very beautiful letter from him, dated September 15, 1956. He wrote that he had found a little Primitive Baptist Church in a small town in Texas and had joined. But the sentence in the letter that leaped out at me was this one: "My health is good, and I am at peace with everybody and everything." I could not help thinking of those words again when, a few months later, I observed his funeral over national television. How wonderful it is for a man to give his heart to Jesus Christ and become a Christian. I see fame and honor, glory and popularity when I go to Washington and see a two hundred million dollar building erected which bears the name of Sam Rayburn. But I know that success is not everything. Things vanish. We cannot measure life merely from the standpoint of success.

A Spiritual Scale

If we cannot measure life from the standpoint of success, we must measure life spiritually. We must put some spiritual weights upon the scales. We must measure ourselves in the light of a knowledge of Jesus Christ.

It is a good thing to live a long time. We should take good care of our bodies; they are temples of the Holy Ghost. But what shall it profit us if we live to be as old as Methuselah and leave Jesus Christ out of our lives? Would it not be better for us not to have lived at all?

It must be a fine thing to have money. I thank God for the great benefactors of the race, the great philanthropists and laymen in our churches whom God has blessed with the ability to make money and who recognize that they are stewards of God. They never forget to share their income with others to help carry on the work of the kingdom of God. But what would it profit them if they had all the money in the world and then lost their immortal souls?

It is a great thing to have knowledge, but if we have all the knowledge in the world and do not have a knowledge of Jesus Christ as our Savior, we die in ignorance. A man made a long journey once to visit a world-renowned scholar and asked him a question: "Of all the things that you have learned, what do you regard as the most valuable?" Without hesitating the eminent scholar replied, "Sir, there are two things I have learned in life. The first is, Sir, I am a great sinner; the second is, Sir, Jesus Christ is a great Savior." If we do not learn these two facts, whatever else we learn is not knowledge at all.

What shall it profit a man if he know all about astronomy and not know him who is the bright and morning star?

What shall it profit a man if he know all about biology and not know him who is the life?

What shall it profit a man if he know all about chemistry and know nothing about the alchemy of the cross?

What shall it profit a man if he know all about philosophy and know nothing of him who is the incarnate truth?

Success is fine. All of us should be ambitious. A man isn't worth the salt in his bread who doesn't want to be somebody in life. Pitiable is the person who has no ambition, no motivation, no desire to be something. Yet no matter how successful you may be, there is a difference in success in the world's eyes and success in God's eyes. No matter how successful the world says we have been, if we do not know Jesus Christ as our personal Savior, we are most pitiful failures.

Therefore, the highest values in life are spiritual values. The highest values are those that are found in a man's relationship to Jesus Christ. For many centuries human personality has had an affinity for Jesus. In Jesus Christ we find peace and joy and fellowship and salvation. We long to know him, to have fellowship with him. Here, my friends, is where man is better than a sheep. No sheep can ever say, The eternal is my dwelling place. No sheep can ever say, The Lord is my shepherd, I shall not want. No sheep can ever say, I accept Jesus Christ as my Savior. I will give him my heart. I will follow him. I'll go where he wants me to go and be what he wants me to be.

Man can do that. Man can get right with God. Man can have *at-one-ment* with God through Jesus Christ. Every man needs a self that is fit to live with. How terrible it must be if every time one looks in the mirror he looks in the face of a hypocrite. It is Jesus Christ alone who can make a self fit to live with. Every person needs a faith to live by. I submit to you that faith in Jesus Christ is faith we can live by. Every person needs a mission worth living for. Jesus Christ gives us that mission on earth when we turn our lives over to him to serve him.

Many years ago a tall, slender young Jew entered an old cathedral in Europe. It was one of the most famous of all cathedrals, with an organ yet more famous. The organist who had played the instrument for many years was now old and had been replaced. But he loved the organ as a mother loves her child, and was custodian of the keys. The young man sought out the old man and said to him, "I hear you have a wonderful organ here." The old man's eyes gleamed. "It is the finest in the fatherland, sir." Then the young man said, "I would like to try it. Would you lend me the key?" The old man drew back. "You'll pardon me, sir, but you know it is a wonderful organ and we're very careful of it. I couldn't give the key to a stranger."

"Well, I play some," said the young man, "and I'm very fond of music. I've traveled a good many miles thinking that I might get to touch the keys." Still the old man refused. But the young man continued to persist, and finally the old man reached into his pocket and took out the key and handed it to him, and the young man went and opened the manual, pulled out the stops, turned on the power, and ran his fingers up and down the keys.

The old man leaned against a pillar, wondering how he had let the key get out of his hands. But when the music began, he forgot all about it. It started very soft, like the singing of the west wind in the treetops on a balmy summer evening, and rose higher and higher and rolled out louder and louder. It seemed as if there was a storm and the thunder deafened the old man; the lightning blinded him, and it was as if he were wet with a dripping rain. And finally, the storm was subdued, the thunder silenced, the lightning ceased, the sun came out, and the music got softer and softer like the breathing of a baby in its mother's arms.

When the young man had finished and lowered the lid over

the key board, he returned the key to the old man. Still under the music's spell, the old man asked, "What is your name?" Modestly, the young man replied, "My name is Felix Mendelssohn, sir." The old man's eyes filled with tears. "To think," he said, "the master is here and I refused him the key!"

Yes, the Master is here. He has been here through all the difficult circumstances, for where two or three are gathered together in his name, there he is in their midst. And he is asking for the key to your life.

Every person may be likened to a great and beautiful organ, with high notes, low notes, heavenly notes, ugly notes, harmony, and dissonance. There is only One whose hand can touch the keyboard. His name is Jesus Christ. Won't you give him the key to your life and let him be the great Musician of your soul?

7.
The Great Salvation

HEBREWS 2:3

"How shall we escape, if we neglect so great salvation?" (v. 3).

We search the world for truth. We cull
The Good, the true, the beautiful,
From graven stone and written scroll,
And all the old flower-fields of the soul;
And, weary seekers of the best,
We come back laden from the quest,
To find that all the sages said
Is in the Book our mothers read.

— JOHN GREENLEAF WHITTIER

If you could have but one book in the entire world, which book would you choose? Without one moment's hesitation, I would choose the Bible. The Bible is more than one book; it is sixty-six books, which make one book. In these 66 books, there are some 1,189 chapters. Three of these 1,189 chapters tell us where we came from; 1,186 tell us where we're going. The Bible is not concerned about where we came from, but it is tremendously concerned about where we are going to spend

In God's great book we find many soul-searching questions. Many of them are still applicable to us today. The Bible is hardly opened before we find God's first question: "Adam . . . where art thou" (Gen. 3:9)? God wanted to know why Adam was hiding. He is still asking why man wants to hide from him in sin.

Farther on, God asks Cain, "Where is Abel thy brother? . . . What has thou done? the voice of thy brother's blood crieth unto me from the ground" (4:9-10). Again man hides in shame.

In the book of Job God asks a question for eternity: "If a man die, shall he live again" (14:14)?

And in the New Testament, "What shall it profit a man, if he shall gain the whole world, and lose his own soul? Or what shall a man give in exchange for his soul" (Mark 8:36-37)?

Again, regarding eternity: "What shall the end be of them that obey not the gospel" (1 Peter 4:17)?

We know the answers to these questions, for God himself has answered them throughout the Bible. But there is one question asked in the New Testament which cannot be answered. It is God's unanswerable question. We find it in Hebrews. No preacher nor theologian can answer it. The angels of heaven and the demons of hell cannot answer it. Neither the most brilliant lawyer nor the leading doctor knows the answer, nor does the most accomplished scientist or inventor. God, Jesus Christ, and the Holy Spirit tell us that there is no answer to this question. Souls in prison know that there is no answer to it.

What is this unanswerable question? It is our text: "How shall we escape if we neglect so great salvation?" If we escape this great salvation which God has provided, there is no other. "There is no other name given under heaven whereby we must be saved," except in the name of the blessed Jesus Christ. There is no other plan of salvation. If we reject this one, there is no other for us.

Let us consider each word of this great text.

A Look at the Text

How, the writer asks, shall we escape? Whoever the author of the epistle of Hebrews was — whether it was Paul, or Apollos — he thought of every possible way of escape. He scanned the horizon, trying desperately to find another way. *How?* he asked, and heard the answer echo, *Impossible.* There is no way.

Notice that he says, How shall *we* escape? not, how shall *they?* "We" means you and I. It means every human soul. How shall each of us escape? It is a personal question, pointed directly at our hearts. God is speaking to us individually.

Note the word *escape.* This word implies that there is something we must escape from; it implies danger, peril, death, destruction, punishment, or the bondage of sin. How shall we escape the penalty of sin? How shall we escape the damnation of hell? How shall we be delivered from the bondage and slavery of sin? How shall we escape if we do not accept this plan of salvation?

"*If* we neglect . . ." The little word *if* is used 1,522 times in the Bible. It is a weak word, but it is fraught with eternity; it is a turning point. There can be no if in God's love.

Neglect. What a sad, tragic word this is. It tells us why there are people who are lost. The majority of people no doubt want to be saved; they want to be Christians; they'd like to have fellowship with God and do his will. But they neglect, they postpone, they delay, they procrastinate. They plan, expect, hope to be Christians, but they delay. And because they delay, they walk the road to destruction, which is paved with good intentions.

Felix needed Christ, and Paul reasoned with him of righteousness, of temperance, and of judgment to come. And Felix trembled and answered, "Go thy way for this time; when I have a more convenient season, I will call for thee." But so far as the record shows, Felix never called for Paul again.

There are many people like that, who never have a more convenient season. So what will happen? If you neglect to feed yourself, you will starve to death. If you neglect your garden, the weeds will take it over. If you neglect your home, you will lose your home; if you neglect your business, you will lose it also. If you neglect to exercise, you will lose the use of your arms or limbs. If you neglect yourself as a Christian, you may become a spiritual pygmy. Certainly, my friends, we must not neglect.

Then I would have you look at this great word *so*. "*So* great salvation." The author of Hebrews was a master of language. He tried to find an adjective adequate to describe salvation, but his marvelous vocabulary failed him. He could only think of one little word, the word *so*.

Finally, the word *salvation* is a thrilling word; what greater word is there? One of America's greatest preachers wrote a book on the great words of the English language. He mentioned many beautiful and wonderful words—*home, mother, faith, repentance, forgiveness, love, kindness, prayer,* and *heaven*. I would have chosen the word *salvation* as a topic for one chapter, for salvation is such an important word. It means to be preserved from destruction.

Someone has said that the world's greatest word is creation. It is not creation, but *re*-creation. It is not generation, but *re*generation. It is not version, but *con*version. All the work of creation cannot be compared to the work of re-creation. Someone has said that God did not shed one drop of blood nor one tear in the creation of the world, but that our Lord Jesus Christ shed his own precious blood on the cross for sinners and wept over their sins.

"How shall we escape if we neglect so great salvation?"

Why Salvation Is Great

Salvation is great because of the magnitude of time involved. Salvation is eternal, everlasting, never-ending. It lasts, not for a day, a week, a month, a year, for ten years, or a thousand years, or a million years. It lasts forever. Salvation is not sufficient unless it is of endless duration. We read that he became unto them that obey him the author of eternal salvation (See Heb. 5:9). An eternal God is Lord of an eternal salvation. We're glad that we're not saved just for a little while.

It's not a small salvation. He loves us with an everlasting love and saves us with an everlasting salvation. He says, "I give unto them eternal life; and they shall never perish, neither shall any man pluck them out of my [Father's] hand" (John 10: 28).

When William MacNeill Poteat, Sr., was dying at Duke University Hospital, a friend went into his room, and it is reported that Dr. Poteat said, "I have just been thinking of what I want put on my tombstone." His friend asked if he had decided, and he said, "Yes. 'Forever with the Lord.' "

Salvation is great because it is salvation that means that we are forever with the Lord. That is an everlasting salvation.

Then, too, salvation is great because it is costly. Consider the cost of war, in billions of dollars and billions of lives. When you stand over the grave of one whose life has been lost in war, you cannot help but think about the cost of war. Visit our bases around the world, or ask any mother or father who has lost a son, and you will get a faint glimpse of the cost of war.

Salvation cost God the Lord Jesus Christ. Words fail to describe what it cost Jesus himself. It cost him condescension. He left his home in glory and came into this sin-blighted world and made himself of no reputation, took upon himself the form of a servant, and was found in the likeness of men, humbled himself, and became obedient unto death, even the death of the cross. At the foot of the cross we see his broken hands and side, his head and feet. We see him despised, rejected, maligned, misrepresented, belittled. We see him wounded for our transgressions, bruised for our iniquities, the chastisement of our peace upon him, bearing our stripes. What a terrible, tragic cost! It was a great price for the great victory of bringing us forgiveness of sin, deliverance from judgment, everlasting life, and the peace of God forever. We are not able to comprehend the cost. Eternity alone will reveal it.

Salvation is costly. It cost God to lift us out of the darkness and depths of despair into the glorious light and liberty of the sons of God. Salvation is so great that only the mind of God could conceive it; only the love of God could provide it; only the power of God could accomplish it. We can say: with Elvina M. Hall

> Jesus paid it all,
> All to Him I owe;
> Sin had left a crimson stain,
> He washed it white as snow.

My friends, it is a great salvation too because it is a complete salvation. God did not start the work of salvation and then give up, turn away, and leave it half finished. Every time I see Stone Mountain in Atlanta I cannot help but wonder why it is that the sculptor who began that carving of Robert E. Lee, Jefferson Davis, and Stonewall Jackson in stone did not finish the job. For years upon years it has stood unfinished.

I'm glad that Jesus finished the job of salvation at Calvary. He didn't start it and then leave it. He didn't get halfway there and then back out. He died to save us from sin to righteousness, from selfishness to magnanimity, from littleness to greatness, from defeat to triumph, from night to day. He died to save our souls, our lives, our bodies, our brains, our influence, our personality. He died to save us to all that is noble, true, and blessed. He died to save us from the past, no matter what our past has been; to save us from the present for the future. We do not have to fear death or judgment or eternity any longer because we have this great salvation. The tumultuous work of God is complete.

One day Jeremiah Taylor picked up a pamphlet entitled "The Finished Work of God," and asked, "What is finished?" Then it dawned on him that the work of salvation was finished. He said, "There's nothing left for me to do but accept it, because God has done it all."

Yes, my friends, God's is a finished work, and his is a great salvation because it is finished. Jesus said, "I have glorified thee on the earth: I have finished the work which thou gavest me to do" (John 17:4). Because he finished it completely, it saves us completely.

The Only Salvation

This salvation — which is eternal, costly, and complete — is the *only* salvation. Many supposed substitutes for salvation are available. Many people try other methods. Some think that they can be saved by church membership; some think that baptism will save them; some think that taking the Lord's Supper will save them. Some think that by being members of a civic club, by rendering service, by doing good deeds, by giving, by practicing the Golden Rule, by being members of certain fraternities that they will be saved. I belong to some of the greatest fraternities in the world. I am very proud of my Masonry. There is much in it that is inspiring, beautiful, and that ought to make us better men. But Masonry has never taught, and never will teach, that it saves any man from sin. It does not offer any way of salvation.

One of the greatest preachers I ever knew was Ellis Fuller of South Carolina, who was a pastor in Atlanta for fourteen years. When Dr. Fuller was a young pastor in South Carolina, he once pitched a tent that would seat six thousand persons on the church grounds, and held a revival for his own people there for about three weeks. He tells this story in a sermon entitled "Prepare to Meet Thy God," in his book of evangelistic sermons.

One day a young man came and asked him to drive about thirteen miles out into the country to see a man he was interested in. Dr. Fuller explained that he would like to go, but that he needed to work on his sermon for that night's revival. But the young man persuaded him of the seriousness of the situation, and Dr. Fuller agreed to go.

When they arrived, they found the man lying on a bed on a

side porch. It was a hot summer day, and his voice was hoarse and he was breathing fast. He was very weak. Dr. Fuller went straight to the point. "Mr. Pinson, I've come to talk to you about your soul. I want you to accept Christ. Are you ready to go?"

"I hope I'm ready," he answered.

"Upon what are you basing your hopes?" asked Dr. Fuller. And the man explained that he had tried to observe the Golden Rule all of his life. He had been a good citizen, and was known by his neighbors as honest. He had always led the battles for better schools, better roads, and a better community. He had lived a life above reproach. He even called in his daughter and his wife, who both assured Dr. Fuller that he had been the best father and husband a family could ask for.

Then Dr. Fuller said to him, "I would be untrue to you if I did not say that if that is all the basis of your hope, you haven't a semblance of a chance to be saved. Have you ever accepted Christ as your Savior? Have you ever repented of your sins? believed in him?"

Mr. Pinson answered that he had never been able to do that. But then, like a drowning man reaching out for a straw, he said, "This is serious. I know my condition; I've got to go. Tell me plainly what it all means." Dr. Fuller told him that Christ loved him and died for him, and then asked him to pray. And as they bowed their heads together in prayer, the Holy Spirit did what he always does. The man's face was illuminated with a heavenly light, and he accepted Jesus Christ's offer of salvation.

In less than a week Dr. Fuller went back to lead the man's funeral.

Salvation is not a trifling matter. A man is saved if he knows Christ, and he is hopelessly lost if he doesn't. There is only one Savior, and he saves only those who will let him. Yes, there are many substitutes for the real thing, but there is no other way of escape. There are not many ways to heaven; there is only one way. Jesus said, "I am the way. Walk ye in it."

A lady one day kept asking if she were on the right train. Finally she asked the conductor, "Are you sure I'm on the right train?" He said, "Yes, lady, you're on the right train." She said, "You just can't imagine how much it means to me to be on the right train. I'm going home."

Are you, my friends, on the right train? Are you on the right track? All other ways lead elsewhere; all other plans fail. But if you trust in Jesus Christ as your Savior, you're on the right track and the way leads home. "For neither is there salvation in any other, for there is none other name under heaven given among men whereby we must be saved." Ours is a great salvation, because it is the *only* salvation. If we miss it, we miss everything and we would do better to miss everything than to miss this pearl of great price. Priscilla J. Owens expressed the joy of salvation in this song:

Waft it on the rolling tide:
Jesus saves! Jesus saves!
Tell to sinners far and wide:
Jesus saves! Jesus saves!
Sing ye island of the sea;
Echo back, ye ocean caves;
Earth shall keep her jubilee:
Jesus saves! Jesus saves!

What will you do without this great salvation? Will you accept it or neglect it? "How shall ye escape if ye neglect so great salvation?"

8. The Call of the Cross

1 CORINTHIANS 1:21-25

"But we preach Christ crucified" (v. 23).

On a magnificent piece of property covering fourteen and one half acres of a high, wooded hill stands a beautiful French Gothic church with a tower 165 feet from the ground. On top of that tower is a huge copper cross, eight feet by five feet, highlighting Atlanta's skyline.

That church is my church, one of the most beautiful sights in the world to me.

When it was being built, I wanted to have on film a record of its construction. As progress was made, I shot the scenes on my movie camera. When the time came for the crew to put the cross on the tower, one of the men called me. When I went over, there lay the cross on the ground, with a rope attached to it. Some of the men were on the ground lifting the cross, and some were up on the roof pulling at the rope.

I watched that cross go dangling through the sky, and when it reached its destination, I saw one man reach out and grapple with it as he tried to place it in its position. It swayed to the left and to the right, and finally it fell into its socket.

As I stood watching, it was as though I heard and saw the flesh tear from the hands and feet of the Son of God. As I thought about the death of the Lord Jesus Christ on that cross for my sins, tears welled up in my eyes and streamed down my cheeks. And I dedicated myself once again to the preaching of the cross of the Lord Jesus Christ.

In the words of Paul:

> For after that in the wisdom of God the world by wisdom knew not God, it pleased God by the foolishness of preaching to save them that believe. For the Jews require a sign, and the Greeks seek after wisdom: but we preach Christ crucified, unto the Jews a stumblingblock, and unto the Greeks foolishness; but unto them which are called, both Jews and Greeks, Christ the power of God, and the wisdom of God. Because the foolishness of God is wiser than men; and the weakness of God is stronger than men (1 Cor. 1:21-25).

The cross, my friends, is the most conspicuous symbol in Christianity. We build our churches traditionally in the form of a cross. We carve the cross on our pulpits and on our pews, and place it on our towers. We magnify the cross of the Lord Jesus Christ.

If you were to tear out the pages of your hymnbook on which there are hymns about the cross, you would mutilate your hymnbook. If you were to tear out the pages of the New Testament which speak about the cross, you would be partially destroying it also, because passage after passage tells us about the death of the Lord Jesus Christ.

The Cross Condemns Sin

Christ was lifted up on his cross for our sins. In John Masefield's book entitled *The Trial of Jesus,* the wife of Pontius Pilate asks the centurion, "What do you think of Jesus?" The centurion replies, "I think that any man who is willing to die on the cross for his convictions will win followers." And when she asked whether he thought the man called Christ was dead, the centurion replied, "No, my lady." "Where is he, then?" "Cut loose in the world where neither Greek nor Roman can stop his truth."

A group of air force chaplains sitting in a hotel lobby in Seoul, Korea, were discussing their favorite painting. They agreed that if they had to select one, it would be the picture of the little boy pointing to a cross on the lapel of a chaplain's uniform.

The hand of a child, his finger pointing to the cross — that is the message of this chapter.

In a military hospital in the Philippines a lad lay dying. This young man said to the chaplain: "Please do me a favor. Get me a cross and put it in my hands. Let me die with a cross in my hands." The chaplain had some difficulty finding a cross, but when he did, he put it in one of the boy's hands and a copy of the New Testament in the other. And that lad died, clinging to the cross with one hand and the New Testament with the other.

If you want something you can cling to, reach for the cross. In life and in death it will be an anchor for your soul. The call of the cross is the clarion call of God. It stigmatizes sin. It tells us that there is something wrong with the world in which we live. It tells us that sin has cursed and warped and blighted and ruined the world in which we live. Medicine is unable to cure sin. Education is unable to teach it the way. Silence has been unable to eradicate it. Magicians have been unable to get rid of it. That abominable thing called sin is what killed the Lord of glory, insulted God's holy majesty, infected God's gracious spirit, trampled under foot his laws, spit in the face of his Son, and nailed Jesus Christ to the cross.

All the darkness, disease, despair, degradation, disorder, and death in the world is the fault of sin. It is a cancer which gnaws at the vitals of humanity. It is a poison in the mind, an opiate in the heart, a frenzy in the imagination, and a blackness which infests man's whole moral being. Sin is a viper.

Have you ever seen a python? A friend once showed me one that had been brought to this country from India. There it lay, curled up in the corner of its cage, looking rather innocent. But when a thirty-pound pig was dropped in the cage, that python wrapped itself like lightning around that pig and tightened on with a vice-like grip. We heard several little squeals, and then that python unravelled itself and laid that pig out on the floor of the cage, lifeless.

What a terrible sight that was! Yet ten times worse is the reality of the fact that there are men and women and boys and girls who are caught in the coils of Satan, and he crushes the spiritual life out of them.

If you examine the life of the blackest criminal, search the slums of the greatest cities, go down to the lowest depths of hell itself, you will not find so vile a picture of sin as you find when you come to the foot of the cross. At the foot of the cross you find sin in its working clothes, murdering the Son of God. It is the iniquitous business of sin to crucify God. Sin is homicidal. Sin is suicidal. But worst of all, sin is deicidal. Sin would climb up to the heights of heaven and grab God off his throne and murder him. And that is what sin did when sin crucified the Lamb of God. Sin never accomplished a more diabolical plan than when it killed Jesus.

The cross is meaningless unless you and I see its relationship to sin. Some time ago, in one of their worldwide conferences, the Roman Catholics vindicated the Jews from killing the Lord Jesus. That action seems to have brought a great deal of satisfaction to our Jewish friends. But in reality, none of us is vindicated because all of us are guilty. All of us had a part in putting Jesus Christ to death, because he died for your sins and mine.

My sins laid open to the rod,
The back which from the law was free,
And the eternal Son of God
Bore the stripes once due to me.

The Cross Reveals Love

The cross of Jesus Christ is not only a sin-condemning cross. It is a love-revealing cross. At the foot of the cross we see love as we see it nowhere else in the world. We see it at its zenith, at its best, at its noblest — a love that is beyond man's imagination. When God made man, he made him in his own image. He took all of his own moral excellences and fashioned them into a crown, and put that crown on the brow of man, and put that man in the garden of Eden. And Satan came by and dipped his arrow deep into sin's poison and aimed it straight at the heart of man, and man went stumbling and staggering and sinning down the road to hell. And God Almighty looked down with a broken heart and saw man's plight. He sent his prophets and his lawmakers and his preachers that man might see that God is and loves and cares. But man went right on down the road to hell.

And then one day with a broken heart, God walked out into that beautiful garden paradise, and looking down upon the sinfulness of man, said, "I know what I'm going to do." He reached over into his beautiful garden and picked the most beautiful flower that blossomed there. He plucked the Rose of Sharon and the Lily of the Valley. He fashioned them into a gorgeous bouquet, and with hands of love and cords of mercy he let that bouquet down into the little town of Bethlehem. They looked at that bouquet and read, "For God so loved the world that he gave his only begotten Son, that whosoever believeth on him should not perish, but have everlasting life."

The cross is a window through which we see into the heart of God. If you have wondered whether anybody loves you, come to the foot of the cross; for that is where you will see how much God loves you. His is a love beyond any love that man has ever known, because Christ shed his blood for you. That is how much he loved you.

The cross is a love-revealing cross.

The Cross Redeems Man

The cross is a gloriously redeeming cross.

All over the world there are people who hunger for God. In the Shinto and Buddhist temples in Japan, I have seen how they combine various teachings and philosophies and try to practice them, searching for God, groping in the darkness. In Taiwan I've seen them throw money into the holy fires, trying to send it on to their departed loved ones. I've seen them buy paper houses and put them into the flames in order to send their loved ones a home to live in in the hereafter. And I've seen them throw something that looked like sandals on the floor to determine God's answer to their prayers. Everywhere people are hungry for God.

A great French philosopher once said to Thomas Carlyle, "I'm going to organize a new religion, and it shall be known as positivism. And in a few years, everyone will accept this new religion." And Carlyle replied, "All you'll have to do is live as no man ever lived, speak as no man ever spoke, die as no man ever died, be buried, and rise again, and the world will accept your religion." Not positivism, nor atheism, nor agnosticism, nor any other religion could survive as Christianity has survived, because none would have the power of the cross. We do not need a new religion; we *have* a good religion. We have the way of the cross, and a faith that centers in the cross of Jesus Christ is an all-sufficient faith — adequate, soul-certain, and soul-satisfying.

At the foot of the cross

> There is a fountain filled with blood
> Drawn from Immanuel's veins;
> And sinners plunged beneath that flood,
> Lose all their guilty stains.

Some people may find those words by William Cowper repulsive, but they are merely symbolic of the outpouring of his life for us. If any man — no matter who he is nor how far he's gone in sin — will come to the foot of the cross and repent of his sins, through faith in Jesus Christ he will be saved. The way of the cross leads home.

In London there is a square known as Charing Cross. One day a little girl got lost and couldn't find her way home. As she sat on an old curbstone, crying her heart out, a policeman came along. He put his arm around her and asked her name.

She didn't know. In fact, she could give him no information at all. The policeman was perplexed, not knowing what to do, until the child said, "But if you'll take me to the Cross, I can find my way home." The way of the cross leads home.

The ground is wondrously level at the foot of the cross. There's room there for all. We sing these words of J. Hussey:

I stood alone at the bar of God,
    In the hush of the twilight dim,
And faced the question that pierced my heart:
    "What will you do with Him?
Crowned or crucified? which shall it be?"
    No other choice was offered to me.

I looked on the face so marred with tears
    That were shed in His agony;
The look in His kind eyes broke my heart,
    'Twas full of love for me:
"Crowned or crucified," it seemed to say;
    "For or against me — choose thou today."

He held out His loving hands to me,
    While He pleadingly said, "Obey!
Make Me thy choice, for I love thee so!"
    I could not say him nay:
Crowned, not crucified, this must not be;
    No other way was open to me.

I knelt in tears at the feet of Christ,
    In the hush of the twilight dim,
And all that I was, or hoped, or sought,
    Surrendered unto Him:
Crowned, not crucified, my heart shall know
    No king but Christ who loveth me so.

Elizabeth Cheney has said that at times she was disturbed by a cry in the middle of the night. On one occasion she got up and went out and there she saw Jesus on his cross. Unable to bear seeing him suffer, she offered to help remove the nails from his hands and feet. He refused but said: "There is one thing you can do for me. You can go and tell every man, woman, boy, and girl in the world that there is a man upon a cross who can't come down until they come to take him down."

When we repent of our sins and believe on the Lord Jesus, we take the nails out of his hands and bring him great and everlasting joy. For more "joy shall be in heaven over one sinner that repenteth, more than over ninety and nine just persons, which need no repentance" (Luke 15:7).

Only at the foot of the cross will we find such salvation!

9. Hungers of the Human Heart

JOHN 6:35

"I am the bread of life" (v. 35).

Hunger and thirst are innate in every human being. All mankind hungers. All men everywhere hunger for what they do not deserve.

There is a hunger peculiar to the believer, who says with the psalmist, "As the hart panteth after the water brooks, so panteth my soul after thee" (42:1). There is also a hunger characteristic of the unbeliever, to whom Isaiah says, "Wherefore do ye spend money for that which is not bread? and your labour for that which satisfieth not?" (55:2)

It is about these hungers that I wish to speak.

Hunger for Food

Perhaps the deepest, most painful hunger of all is the hunger for bread. The shout of "fire" on the streets is nothing compared to the agony heard in the cry for bread. That cry has never been louder nor more pronounced that it is at present, despite our assumed affluence. Even in this land of plenty, someone telephones me almost every week to say they do not have food to eat, clothes to wear, or shelter. Many of them make other requests. Almost every week there are transients who come by begging. Almost all of them are hungry. All of them are glad whenever I make it possible for them to get food.

I shall never forget the starvation I have seen in traveling around the world. I can never forget those lean fingers and hands, those undernourished, sad-looking little bodies in Hong Kong and India. I shall always remember mothers with babies in their arms who begged; large crowds of little children who ran after us; young women, old women . . . how my heart went out to every one of them! We are told that half of the world is starving to death. Half of the world never knows what it means to lie down at night having had three square meals. Hunger for food is sharper than any fear of the sword.

The problem is real, not only in India and other foreign lands, but in our own country as well. There is no doubt what President Nixon had in mind when he laid down the wage-price freeze. He is eager to see that there is food in every pantry of every home in the United States, that every person is employed, that every person makes a good wage. Certainly this is a problem of our nation and a problem of the church, and it is something that Christianity is concerned about.

The Bible tells of a seven-year famine in Egypt, when in desperation the people brought gold to Joseph to purchase grain. When the money was all gone, when the flocks and herds and lands were all gone — when they had nothing else with which to buy grain — they began to barter themselves for bread. There is pictured a group of noble men and women in all of their finery appealing to Joseph for help. "There is not ought left in the sight of my lord, but our bodies, and our lands: . . . buy us and our land for bread" (cf. Gen. 47:13-25).

Similarly, Esau's attitude was, "What's a birthright if you cannot get food for your stomach?" Food is a necessity. It is the fuel that produces energy for our bodies. Man has to work for bread by the sweat of his brow, and he will fight or steal for it if necessary. Man's appetite must be satisfied.

One of the greatest miracles our Lord ever performed was the miracle of the feeding of the five thousand. When Philip saw the size of the crowd, he came to Jesus and said, "From whence can a man satisfy these men with bread here in the wilderness?" And Jesus asked him to seat the multitude. Then Andrew, Peter's brother, came and advised Jesus that there was a lad in the multitude who had five loaves and two fishes, and when these were turned over to Jesus, he wrought a mighty miracle. Everyone was satisfied, and there were twelve basketfuls left over.

The people thought of Jesus as a bountiful Lord. They hoped that he would go on giving them bread. But Jesus was less concerned with their physical nourishment — as important as that was — than he was with their spiritual enrichment. He tells them in John 6:55: "My flesh is meat indeed, and my blood is drink indeed." These are ailments which nourish the body far better, and invigorate the soul for immortality.

God has placed us in a world of plenty, overflowing with good things to eat. But because man sins there is starvation. Many of us fail to use what God has given us, and consequently there are multiplied millions who go hungry. But there are also multiplied millions of persons who go hungry spiritually. Jesus said, "I am the bread of life: he that cometh to me shall never hunger; and he that believeth on me shall never thirst."

Hunger for Knowledge

Another of the deepest and most profound hungers of mankind is the hunger for knowledge. Man has an insatiable thirst for knowledge. He searches for light all his life, a search that is indeed laudable, for the most civilized people are the most advanced in knowledge.

Nevertheless, unless we have wisdom to control our knowledge, it will be to us like tainted food; it will poison the body disastrously. There is a wide strain of knowledge which has been harmful to our faith. Edison once suggested that we ought to quit our inventions for twenty years until people become good enough to learn to use the inventions they already have. We know now — perhaps better than ever in this highly scientific age of astonishing inventions — that Edison was right. We must have devotion commensurate with our scientific achievement. We must have faith, religion, consecration. We must have time to let our selves catch up with our minds, our bodies, our knowledge. Is it not true that there are those who, though ever learning, never come to a knowledge of the truth? Are there not many who have spent years studying in the great universities and collecting information in the vast libraries of the land who have never known the greatest reality of all? Are there not many who know much about many things but very little about God?

Many years ago a pulpit committee came from Liberty, Missouri, to the little town of Benson, South Carolina, to hear me preach. I didn't know they were there. They went back to Liberty and the next Sunday extended a call to me to become the pastor of their church. I recall getting on the train and going to St. Louis, then on to Kansas City where I was met by a group of gracious people from Liberty. In my visiting with them, I remember saying to Dr. Herbert, who was then president of William Jewell College, that I was really frightened to become their pastor because there were so many Ph.D.'s in the congregation. He said to me: "Son, don't worry about these Ph.D.'s. They're all sinners, and they all need the gospel. They may know all about their fields, but they all need to know more about God, and they need a man of God to tell them."

Surely there are Ph.D.'s who know God. Many of them are fine and wonderful Christians. But we can well imagine that there are some who do not know God. Whatever the case, they all have hearts, and they all hunger for God just as we do.

If we do not have the love of God in our hearts, we remain in unhappy and ruinous ignorance. Without this love of Jesus Christ, we must be fools forever. If man wishes to find solid footing, he must stand upon the Rock of Ages. Then he can express with conviction that, whatever else is true or not true, Jesus Christ is the embodied, personalized declaration of reality. As we trust him as our Savior, we become as guided vessels on the sea of life, and sail with a heavenly pilot on board to an eternal home. Jesus said, "If ye continue in my word, then are ye my disciples indeed; and ye shall know the truth, and the truth shall make you free" (John 8:32).

Hunger for Companionship

It is certainly a biological fact that all animals hunger for companionship. We are by nature ·gregarious. Witness the number of clubs to which we belong!

All of mankind seems to hunger for companionship. Some of the sweetest joys of life come from communing with friends. What pleasure is there except in sharing with others? Food tastes better when we eat with others. Few men like to hunt or fish or play golf alone. Friends add spice to our lives. How wonderful it is when we have the right kind of companionship.

But, my friends, just as there is tainted food and tainted knowledge, there is also the wrong kind of company. Someone has said, "If you lie down with dogs, you get up with fleas." Companions *make* a man or a woman; they help to shape his or her character. I wonder if there would be as much juvenile delinquency if parents would safeguard their children's company.

One of the swiftest routes to ruin is bad associates. I am reminded of the story of two men on Brooklyn Bridge. One was about to jump off. The other decided to reason with him and try to dissuade him. Both jumped off! We ought to be very careful about the kind of companions we select.

I shall always be grateful to my high school principal who, when I was a boy, reminded me that one of the most important things I could do in life would be to select good companions.

If we really are hungry in our hearts for companionship, that hunger will never be met until we let Jesus come into our hearts. Jesus is worthy of our friendship; we can love and trust and adore him. He will never deceive us, disappoint us, or lie to us. He will never let us down as friends sometimes do.

How sad it is to be disappointed in a friend! David knew that sadness. He said, "I took sweet counsel with him in the house of the Lord, and yet it was he who betrayed me." Jesus also knew. When Judas came to betray him, he said, "Friend, what thou doest, do quickly."

Jesus is the dearest friend of all. He laid down his life for us, saying: "Greater love hath no man than this, that a man lay down his life for his friends. Ye are my friends, if ye do whatsoever I command you" (John 15:13-14). The joys of this world and fellowship with man cannot be compared with the joys of communion with Jesus Christ. If you have his friendship, you will overflow with joy and never hunger.

Hunger for Beauty

If there is not a hunger for beauty in this world, there should be. Ecclesiastes 3:11 says: "He hath made everything beautiful in his time: also he hath set the world in their heart." God has given us a world of beauty with the faculty to appreciate it. I believe it was Emerson who said, "Beauty is his who can entertain it." Beauty, like truth, is his who can appreciate it.

But alas, my friends, there are too many who are not even able to see it. At the entrance of beautiful Callaway Gardens in Georgia one finds these words: "Remove nothing from the gardens except nourishment for the soul, consolation for the heart, and inspiration for the mind." Those who litter the grounds or deface the scenery evidently have no appreciation for beauty. In Mobile's Bellingrath Gardens visitors are similarly told: "May it not be said, and said to your shame, that all was beauty here until you came."

How beautiful is this world that God has made. Yet as beautiful as the earth is and as much as we admire it, it cannot satisfy our souls. The perception of fragmentary beauty gives us a longing for completeness found only in Jesus Christ. In Christ is true beauty, the beauty of perfect selflessness, sympathy, insight, and love. He is the ultimate beauty of God himself. Why did God make all things beautiful? Perhaps the answer is that he did so in order that infinite loveliness made incarnate in his Son might be the most beautiful of all.

Fair is the sunshine,
Fairer still the moonlight
And all the twinkling, starry host;
Jesus shines brighter, Jesus shines purer
Than all the angels heaven can boast.

Hunger for Love

Man also hungers for love. We recognized this in discussing his hunger for companionship. Love is inherent in humanity. What a man loves has a tremendous effect upon his personality; what he loves tells what he is. Some people love money until they grow cold and metallic inside. Some couples love each other until they grow to look like each other. Love transfigures. It inspires. No man ever achieved greatness without the inspiration of love for someone behind him.

Likewise, many a person's love is poisoned with love of the wrong thing. Love may be dissipated or turned to sin for the pleasures of the world. If we would love to the greatest degree, we must turn our affection to the greatest of all lovers, to him who is love. "God is love, and he that dwelleth in love dwelleth in God and God in him." There is in the human heart that which can never be satisfied until that heart is flooded with the love of God. In the depth of man's heart, there is that which only God can fill.

Bruce Barton has written a parable about two kinds of love. It is called "There Are Two Seas."

> There are two seas in Palestine. One is fresh, and fish are in it. Splashes of green adorn its banks. Trees spread their branches over it, and stretch out their roots to dip of its healing water. Along its shore children play. The river Jordan makes this sea with sparkling water from the hills. So it laughs in the sunshine. And men build their houses near to it, and birds their nests; and every kind of life is happier because it is there.
>
> The river Jordan flows on south into another sea. Here is no splash of fish, no fluttering leaf, no song of birds, no children's laughter. Travelers choose another route, unless on urgent business. The air hangs above its waters and neither man nor beast nor fowl will drink.
>
> What makes this mighty difference in these neighbor seas?
>
> Not the river Jordan. It empties the same water into both.
>
> Not the soil in which they lie. Not the country round about. This is the difference:
>
> The Sea of Galilee receives, but does not keep the Jordan.
>
> For every drop that flows into it another drop flows out.
>
> The giving and receiving go on in equal measure.
>
> The other sea is selfish, hoarding its income jealously.
>
> Every drop it gets, it keeps. The Sea of Galilee gives and lives.
>
> This other sea gives nothing. It is called the Dead Sea.
>
> There are two kinds of seas in Palestine.
>
> There are two kinds of people in the world.

If a sea has no outlet, it stagnates. Is this not what happened to the Dead Sea? Is this not what happens to us when there is no outlet for our love? If man's heart has no outlet, then love stagnates. But we will find that the more we love, the more love we have to give.

Love is only brightest when it proceedeth
to truer, deeper Life above,
Human love is sweetest where it leadeth
to a more Divine Perfect Love.

Hunger for Righteousness

Mankind also hungers and thirsts after goodness and holiness.

We all have consciences. Most want to keep their consciences clear. Most would like to be able to lie down at night and sleep peacefully. No fire burns hotter than a quilty conscience. Lady Macbeth, who murdered her husband, cried out: "Ha! What hands are here? They pluck out mine eyes. Will all great Neptune's ocean wash this blood clean from my hand?" Her hand was clean, but there was blood on her heart and conscience. Only the blood of the Lamb could cleanse such spots.

Perhaps you feel that you cannot live in the future without living in the past. I have good news for you. You do not have to remain what you have been. You can be different. You can be better than you are. Christ died for you. You say, I want to be pure; I want to be holy; I want to be good. If you repent of your sins, confessing and forsaking them, believe on the Lord Jesus Christ, commit yourself to him and trust in him; his grace will save you. He will make you a new creation in Christ. Your troubled conscience will find peace if you will let Christ come into your heart.

What is your standard of righteousness? Jesus said to his disciples, "Except your righteousness shall exceed the righteousness of the scribes and Pharisees, ye shall in no case enter into the kingdom of heaven" (Matt. 5:20). Does your view of righteousness consist in being good, or being baptized, or giving a tithe, or doing all you can for the poor, or living a good moral life? All of these are important, but this is not the righteousness we really want. We have no righteousness if this is all the righteousness we have. But if we can say, "My righteousness is but as filthy rags; the only goodness I have was bought for me through Jesus Christ on Calvary's cross," then we have real righteousness. Jesus says, "Your righteousness is of me." If you trust in anything else for salvation — if you think you can save yourself — you're wrong. But if you can say — first, last, and always — "I trust only in Jesus," and rely on him with all your heart, then you're right. And you can say,

> Jesus, thy blood and righteousness
> My beauty are, my glorious dress.

"Blessed are they which do hunger and thirst after righteousness, for they shall be filled" (Matt. 5:6).

Hunger for Happiness

Everybody wants to be happy. But happiness cannot be obtained directly; it is the by-product of a satisfied hunger and a quenched thirst.

Man seeks happiness in various ways. Some think that they can find happiness by listening to loud music. It seems that by doing this they try to keep from hearing themselves think. Others say that they will be happy when they make a lot of money. They think they can buy anything they want. But riches are not everything, for they do not really satisfy nor make a person happy. One of my friends told me about a man who put $350,000 in a safety deposit box in the bank and then worried himself to death because he was not getting any interest out of it. A man's life does not consist of the abundance of his possessions. In fact, they can become a burden and a master unless one knows Jesus Christ.

Others say they'll be happy when they quit work, sit down and rest, and do nothing. But some of the most miserable people on earth are idle.

Some say a man's happiness is measured by his accomplishments. It was William Hazlitt who once said: "I loitered my life away, reading books, looking at pictures, going to plays, hearing, thinking, or writing on what pleased me best. I have wanted one thing to make me happy; but wanting that, I have wanted everything."

Still others say, I'll be happy when I have power, prestige, honor, fame. But the supremely great are often the supremely lonely. One of the most genial and affable of United States Presidents once admitted that it was no fun being President. Napoleon Bonaparte, who gained fame as a military genius, is said to have remarked that he did not have a single friend.

No, my friends, we do not gain happiness from the standpoint of fame, honor, wealth, or glory. This earth, with all of its wealth and power and fame, cannot satisfy the hunger of the human heart for happiness.

The secret of real happiness is found in the possession of real joy. There can be no genuine joy except that which comes as the result of fellowship and friendship with Christ. In him we must live and move and have our being, or else we do none of these. The happiest people I have known are those who have been the busiest for Christ. Religion in the heart makes one happy, and out of the heart are the issues of life. As a man thinketh in his heart, so is he happy or unhappy. Robert Burns expressed it in this verse:

It's no in books, it's no in lear,
    To make us truly blest;
If happiness has not her seat
    And center in the breast
We may be wise, or rich, or great,
    But never can be blest.

To whom, then, shall we go to satisfy our hungers? The Bible says, "Thou hast the words of eternal life." The touch of his hand upon ours is enough; Christ alone can satisfy. "Whoso trusteth in the Lord, happy is he" (Prov. 16:20).

Satisfaction for Man's Hungers

All of us hunger for bread, knowledge, companionship, beauty, love, righteousness, and happiness. God has the answers for all hunger, and God's answer is Jesus Christ. "My God shall supply all your need according to his riches in glory by Christ Jesus," wrote Paul (Phil. 4:19). There is nothing we hunger for that God cannot supply. He can meet the deepest cravings of our souls. No key ever fitted a lock better than Christ fits the sinner's heart. He is the all-sufficient Savior, the satisfying Christ.

We want many things; what we need is Jesus. We need pardon; we need cleansing; we need comfort; we need peace; we need life. And Jesus knew whereof he spoke when he said, "Blessed are they which do hunger and thirst after righteousness, for they shall be filled." The tragedies of life come from trying to feed the soul on illegitimate food. The supreme satisfaction of life comes from feeding our souls on the bread of life.

If your soul is starved, Christ will feed it.

If your soul is sick, Christ will heal it.

If your heart is black with sin, Christ can wash it clean.

If you are lost in your sin, Christ can save you.

Why? Because Jesus is God's answer to the cries of hunger in the hearts of all mankind.

10.
The Great Revival

HABAKKUK 3:2

"O Lord, revive thy work in the midst of the years" (v. 2).

The cry of Habakkuk is the anxious cry of an overburdened heart, of one who feels a keen responsibility for the spirituality of his day. His people are in great sorrow. They have forsaken Almighty God. In anguish Habakkuk poured out his troubled soul to God, petitioning for what he believed with all his heart was the only hope for real deliverance. "O Lord," he said, "revive thy work in the midst of the years, . . . in wrath remember mercy."

What work was Habakkuk talking about?

In 1:5 we find God's promise: "I will work a work in your days, which ye will not believe, though it be told you." Habakkuk prayed for a revival of the work of God, for a renewal of his dealing with individuals and with national sins. He shuddered as he thought of how grievous the affliction might be, but passionately prayed that the work might hasten and that God would be merciful.

Over and over we hear this same cry through the ages. In the midst of affliction and distress the psalmist prayed for revival, saying: "Wilt thou not revive us again: that thy people may rejoice in thee" (85:6)? It was wintertime spiritually. The earth was cold, the winds bleak; the trees showed no signs of life; the flowers were withered and gone, and death reigned. But the coming of the spring brought changes; all nature burst forth into new life and wondrous beauty. So the psalmist prayed for spiritual resurrection, a quickening of God's spirit in the midst of his people's desolation. If God would restore again the joy of their salvation, their hearts would rejoice in him.

The great evangelical prophet Isaiah also saw the necessity of revival. He told the people of Judah that God had nourished them, had brought them up as children, and yet they had rebelled against him. He said they were a "sinful nation, a people laden with iniquity, a seed of evildoers, children that are corrupters: they have forsaken the Lord, they have provoked the Holy One of Israel unto anger, they are gone away backward" (1:4). The result of their disobedience was that their hearts were sick and faint, their country was desolate, their cities were burned. God was tired of their multitudes of sacrifices when they were not living sacrificial lives. And the great prophet Isaiah cried out, "Wash you, make you clean; put away the evil of your doings from before mine eyes; cease to do evil; learn to do well; seek judgment, relieve the oppressed, judge the fatherless, plead for the widow. Come now, and let us reason together, . . . though your sins be as scarlet, they shall be as white as snow" (vv. 16-18).

Jeremiah, who was known as the weeping prophet because his face was wet with tears over the sins of his day, cried out and said, "Turn thou us unto thee, O Lord, and we shall be turned; renew our days as of old" (Lam. 5:21). And in 2 Chronicles 7:14 we read the words of the Lord to Solomon: "If my people, which are called by my name, shall humble themselves, and pray, and seek my face, and turn from their wicked ways; then will I hear from heaven, and will forgive their sin, and will heal their land."

These cries are the cries of our own hearts for revival in our day and generation. As desperately as men needed God in the days of Habakkuk, Isaiah, Jeremiah, and the psalmist, these cries were no more fitting then than they are in our day. In deep distress of soul we join in these cries for revival, and we say with the psalmist and with Habakkuk, "O Lord, revive thy work in the midst of the years. Wilt thou not revive us again, that thy people may rejoice in thee?"

The Present Spiritual Crisis

We are experiencing days of special crisis. The word crisis in relation to health means a change in disease which indicates whether a patient will get well — whether he will recover or die. We are in such a crisis today. We hear much about economic recession, and much is being done to try to recover from it. If we as Christians would work as hard as our nation's leaders work to fight for economic revival, we would have one of the greatest spiritual revivals in all of history. What giant efforts are being made to save business, to restore prosperity, to keep down unemployment. Industrial, social, and economic reforms are the order of the day. Whole systems are in the process of revolutionary change. Scientific advance is moving at an ever-quickening pace.

But where are we spiritually?

If nineteenth-century man could come back to earth and see only the advancements of modern-day science, he would say, "This is a new world; I do not recognize it." But if he were to spend time with the people, he would no doubt say, "This is the same old seedy world in which I lived. It is no better." I wonder if this would not be true also of our spiritual condition if Isaiah and Jeremiah and the psalmist returned.

According to Dr. Eual Lawson of the Home Mission Board's Department of Evangelism, Lenin is reported to have said before World War II:

> We will win the Western world without shedding a drop of Russian blood. We will create fear and suspicion; we will work inside by creating racial hatreds, religious antagonisms; we will pit father against son, wife against husband; we will inaugurate campaigns to hate the Jews, and to hate Catholics, and to hate Negroes; we will inspire sit-down strikes and riots; we will plant the seeds of turmoil and we will cover it all with an inflation which will lead to economic disaster until we

> have 14,000,000 unemployed people on the streets of the democratic country of imperialistic America. We will break their economy; we will send their dollar down until it will not be worth ten cents. We will destroy the future security from life insurance, from old-age pensions, until a life annuity that some felt would be substantial for the last of life will buy but a loaf of bread. We will break their currency, we will break their spirit, we will frighten them, we will scare them, we will create political chicanery; we will confuse international diplomacy — WE WILL DO THESE THINGS.

While communism works day and night to accomplish its aims, what are we as Christians doing? Are we fiddling while Rome burns? Are we on a sit-down strike? Are we doing nothing? Many Christians are not even attending church. Many are taking their ease in Zion. Some are saying, These revivals are all bosh.

The truth, my friends, is that the only hope of individual and national deliverance is through revival.

The Need for Revival

The prayer room of our nation's capitol is one of the most beautiful I've ever seen. It is more beautiful because of Brooks Hayes, who was at one time President of the Southern Baptist Convention and who helped bring it about. It houses ten chairs, two kneeling benches, and a beautiful altar with an open Bible pointing to Psalm 16:1: "Preserve me, O God: for in thee do I put my trust." On the altar are two beautiful brass candelabra with seven candles each, and a United States flag to the right. Above the open Bible is a stained glass window with a vase of pink carnations and snapdragons on either side. The window speaks of the religious faith of our nation. George Washington, the father of our country, is on his knees, reminding us of the words from his first inaugural speech, in which he said:

> It would be peculiarly improper to omit in the first official act, my fervent supplications to that Almighty Being who

> rules over the universe, who presides in the councils of nations, and whose providential aids can supply every human defect, that His benediction may consecrate to the liberties and happiness of the people of the United States, a government, instituted by themselves for these essential purposes, and may enable every instrument employed in its administration to execute with success the functions allotted to his charge.

Above all and below are the two sides of the Great Seal of the United States. Above is a pyramid and eye with the Latin phrases, "God has favored our undertakings," and "A new order of the ages is born." Below is the eagle, "E Pluribus Unum," meaning "One from many." Under the seal is a phrase from Lincoln's immortal Gettysburg Address: "This nation under God." The names of the thirteen original states are on scrolls, and the names of the other states are on laurel leaves.

The walls are a pastel blue. The ceiling is the original one with cloud panels trimmed in gold. The rug is a deep blue, and the chapel is illuminated by indirect light. The altar and prayer benches are of white oak. This prayer room is a shrine in which the individual may renew his faith in God and his love for his country.

Entering this prayer room, one feels glad to live in the United States of America. The first clause of the First Amendment to the Constitution, which reads "Congress shall make no law respecting an establishment of religion," is designed not to discourage religion but to ensure equal freedom to all. For various groups, this clause, under the interpretation of the courts, has come to be the basis for separation of church and state. Yet prayer was offered by the great convention which framed our Constitution. By prayer the Congress opens all of its sessions. Through the ministry of chaplains of the great faiths, the men in our armed forces are daily strengthened in will and life. On our coins and on many of our postage stamps we witness our faith in divine providence. Thus Congress provided for its members a quiet place in the nation's capitol where its members may seek the consciousness of God's presence, the light of his guiding, and the strength of his love.

My friend "Fish Bait" Miller invited me to go to this prayer room to meet a group of sixty high-school girls from Houston who were coming on tour of the capitol. As this beautiful group came into the room, I went down on my knees and prayed a prayer out of my heart for them. My prayer was the prayer of Habakkuk: "O Lord, revive thy work in the midst of the years. Wilt thou not revive us again, that thy people may rejoice in thee?"

What we need more than anything else in the world is a genuine revival of religion, a genuine application of spiritual religion to the ways of men. We need a spiritual regeneration of modern life. We need a gracious and genuine revival of the religion of Jesus Christ, a religion that would plant the love of God in the hearts of men and women and boys and girls. The world has never needed Jesus Christ more than now. Christ is God's answer to every problem of the human heart.

Some time ago I was in a revival meeting with Dr. Frederick E. Smith, one of the most beloved pastors I've ever known. He asked me to sit in his car and wait for him, and presently he came back with a yellowed piece of paper, put it in my hands, and said, "Look at that." It was a church letter twenty-five years old. The name had been changed because the woman had been married and had children and grandchildren in that time. She had carried this letter around with her for all these years, without ever having put it in the church.

Why is it that we have so many absentee members? Why is it that we have so many people who leave their memberships at home? Thousands move to our great cities each year. Many of them at one time knew hard times; many of them did not always have the luxuries or the good food that they now have. They have left God at home. They have forgotten him, forsaken him. Many of them are lost who may have once known the Lord. They have lost the joy of their salvation.

How many their excuses are! But these excuses will not hold up in the day of judgment. Some of the excuses given to me in a revival meeting recently in Washington are these:

"I'm just lazy, and I'm not making any excuse for it."

"I would join if my husband would join."

A twelve-year-old boy asked his older brother why their parents didn't attend. The boy said, "They're too busy working to come to church."

A seventy-four-year-old man said that he had drunk a lot of liquor in his day, and now that he had one foot in the grave, he was out of reach of the cross.

One family had posted this sign on their door: "Positively no solicitors." Another read, "Please keep off the grass."

A lady forty years old who had never joined the church said, "I never will join. My husband sees so many people who attend church on Sunday doing what they shouldn't be doing during the week."

A waitress who worked the night shift said, "If I had time I would come to church." I tried to remind her that she's not too busy to die.

Another lady and her husband, who had been in Washington for seventeen years, said she didn't believe in water baptism. "Besides, we're only going to be here for three years and then we're going to Florida to retire. Maybe we'll join somewhere else, but not here."

A seventeen-year-old youngster said, "I'm not satisfied, but I can't make up my mind." I told her she wouldn't do it any younger.

Another said, "If it were not for the children, I'd come."

Another said, "If I had children, I'd certainly come."

Whatever your ridiculous excuses are, drop them! Find God in revival. God does not want you by your inconsistent life to stand in the way of a spiritual awakening.

Have you taken his name in vain? Have you professed faith

in Christ and turned your back on him? Have you been untrue? Have you been unfaithful? Do you say that you are a Christian and live like the devil? Do you take the cup of the Lord's Supper and yet live a worldly life? Do you stay in bed on Sunday morning instead of going to Sunday School? You get out of bed every Monday morning and go to work, or go fishing, or go to see your relatives. Are you too spiritually lazy or indifferent to go to God's house?

How long would you live in the city in which you live if there were no churches? Everyone admitted to me in Washington that they wouldn't live in America if there were no churches. And yet, my friends, these people who do not accept Christ, who do not move their membership, who show no interest in the church whatsoever, are they not helping to destroy America? America is great because of the greatness of her churches.

Do you have time to read the papers? Do you have time for the television shows? Do you have time to go to football and baseball games? to ride in your automobile? to go boating, play golf, play tennis, but have no time for God Almighty? Judgment must begin at the house of God. In proportion to our unholiness, God withholds his blessings. God would best sweep his own temple, his own church, before he can give the community a blessing.

Revival must begin in us, in the church. We as church members must repent of our sins, of our broken vows, of our uncharitable judgments, of our open transgressions of God's laws. We must repent of our failure to adequately represent him. We must repent of our lack of prayer life, resulting in lack of power. We must repent of the shameful way we have shunned God's causes. We must repent of our listlessness, our cruel indifference, our inactivity, our spiritual barrenness, our stinginess. We push others forward but will not go forward ourselves. We want the work of God to be revived, but are unwilling to be revived ourselves. We want the church to maintain worship services, but we will not worship.

One day unless we repent we will live in a Godless, churchless, Christless world, and how deep and bitter our regrets will be. The church of Jesus Christ — more than any other — is a church filled with Laodiceans. "Because," he said, "thou art lukewarm, and neither hot nor cold, I will spew thee out of my mouth." A cold, dead church has no message. A lukewarm church professes to have one, but has no passion, no urgency. It gives a false alarm. May God save our churches from lukewarmness!

There is a devoted, consecrated nucleus in the church who has never forsaken nor forgotten God — the Habakkuks, Isaiahs, Jeremiahs, and others — whose hearts break over sin and corruption. They love the Lord Jesus. They love the church, lost souls, and people everywhere. It is their relatives, their friends, and their neighbors who are lost. How they need Christ. How they need revival. They are strangers to the church and to the cross, strangers to Christ. They are under the curse of sin.

If you believe the Bible, you know that those outside of Christ go where "the worm dieth not and the fire is not quenched." Make haste, my friends, invite them, urge them, pray with them. Remember your Savior's cross. Remember he died for sinners. "Did Christ o'er sinners weep; And shall our cheeks be dry?" William P. Mackay wrote:

We praise thee, O God!
For the Son of Thy love,
For Jesus who died,
And is now gone above.

Revive us again!
Fill each heart with Thy love,
May each soul be rekindled
With fire from above.

11.
The Matchless Name

PHILIPPIANS 2:9-11

"Wherefore God also hath highly exalted him, and given him a name which is above every name" (v. 9).

What's in a name? Almost everything.

A name stands for something: for a person, for character, for honor, for loyalty. What does your name stand for?

The Scriptures tell us, "A good name is rather to be chosen than great riches" (Prov. 22:1). Many years ago a bank went broke is South Carolina. The directors of the bank met and tried to reorganize it. They selected for their president a farmer, and went out to visit him to ask if he would accept the position. He told them he couldn't accept because he didn't have a great deal of money. He wasn't a wealthy man. They replied, "But you have something that's worth far more than money. You have a good name."

If you have a good name, cherish it; defend it; hold it high; let no person drag it in the mire or besmirch it. Live up to your name.

A Sacrificial Name

As important as our own names are, we are not here to talk about them. We are here to think about that name which is above every name. William Hunter has written:

Sweetest note in seraph song,
Sweetest name on mortal tongue,
Sweetest carol ever sung,
Jesus, blessed Jesus.

Take that name from the Word of God and you emasculate the Bible. Take that name from human history, and it is as a tale that is told, full of sound and fury, signifying nothing. Take that name from the human heart, and love is dead. Take that name from the world, and the world is without hope. Take that name from the ministry, and the minister is without a message. Take that name from the church, and the church is without a mission. Take that name from the kingdom, and the kingdom is without a king. His is a name which is above every name: "That at the name of Jesus every knee should bow, of things in heaven, and things in earth, and things under the earth; and that every tongue should confess that Jesus Christ is Lord, to the glory of God the Father" (Phil. 2:10-11).

Several things could be said about the matchless name of Jesus. First, his name is above all others because it is a sacrificial name. His very name means sacrifice.

Sacrifice is one of the most beautiful words in the languages of the world. It embodies all that is good, merciful, and noble. The angel said: "She shall bring forth a son, and thou shalt call his name Jesus: for he shall save his people from their sins" (Matt. 1:21).

His name means captain of salvation. "He was wounded for our transgressions, he was bruised for our iniquities: the chastisement of our peace was upon him; and with his stripes we are healed" (Isa. 53:5).

He is the sacrificial "Lamb of God which taketh away the sin of the world" (John 1:29).

The Scriptures are full of references to Jesus as God's sacrifice upon the altar of the world for redemption of man's sin.

"Forasmuch as ye know that ye were not redeemed with corruptible things, as silver and gold, . . . but with the precious blood of Christ, as of a lamb without blemish and without spot" (1 Pet. 1:18-19).

"Thou wast slain, and hast redeemed us to God by thy blood

out of every kindred, and tongue, and people and nation; and hast made us unto our God kings and priests" (Rev. 5:9-10).

Jesus was "made a little lower than the angels for the suffering of death, crowned with glory and honour; that he by the grace of God should taste death for every man" (Heb. 2:9).

The Scriptures also tell us that he was made perfect by suffering. The song by Elvina M. Hall describes Jesus' sacrifice.

Jesus paid it all,
All to Him I owe;
Sin had left a crimson stain,
He wash'd it white as snow.

Jesus sacrificed his all for us. He died for our sins. He suffered painfully, agonizingly, unflinchingly, heroically. He sweat great drops of blood in the garden of Gethsemane. They spat on him, whipped him with cords of steel, tore his beautiful brow with a crown of thorns, made him walk the cobblestones, and laid a heavy cross upon him. They drove heavy, rusty spikes through his hands and feet. His lips were as parched as the desert sand. They thrust a spear through his side, and when they did, water and blood flowed out, symbolic of a broken heart.

A story is told of a young artist who painted a peculiarly beautiful picture. People who went to view it were amazed at its beauty. One of the reasons for its beauty was that the artist had opened one of his veins and drawn out some of his own blood and mixed it with the paint. He had put his own life's blood into the painting.

That, my friends, is what Jesus did for us. And that is why his name is honey to the mouth, music to the ear, and gladness to the heart. He is the lily of the valley because the rich, red blood of his body was shed for our sins, that the canvas of our lives might be as pure as the morning dew.

A little boy was walking with his father one evening when they happened to see a bright golden star shining in a window.

The little fellow asked what it meant. The father explained that out of that home a son had gone to war, and that son had been killed in battle. The family had placed this star there in his memory. They walked on a little farther and saw two bright stars shining in a window. The boy asked what that meant, and the father explained that two fine boys from that home had given their lives for their country. As they walked on farther, the boy looked up into the sky and pointed to the evening star. "Daddy, I know what that star means," he said. "That star means that God had a Son, and God gave his Son for us."

This is the story of the cross. This is what God did for us, for he was in Christ, reconciling the world unto himself. Isaac Watts wrote:

> See, from His head, His hands, His feet,
> Sorrow and love flow mingled down;
> Did e'er such love and sorrow meet,
> Or thorns compose so rich a crown.

Two years ago it was my privilege to lead in prayer at a meeting of Gold Star Mothers. As I saw these mothers assemble, each of whom had given a son, I thought, How wonderful it is that they know what the word sacrifice means. Jesus knows even more fully what it means, because he laid down his own life for us in holy, loving sacrifice.

An Exalted Name

Jesus' name is a matchless name because it is exalted. "Wherefore God also hath highly exalted him." Again the Scriptures are full of references to this fact.

Long ago Isaiah said, "His name shall be called Wonderful, Counsellor, The mighty God, The everlasting Father, The Prince of Peace. Of the increase of his government and peace there shall be no end" (9:6-7).

The Scriptures also tell us that, in Jesus, the prophecy of

Isaiah was fulfilled, who had said, "They shall call his name Emmanuel, which being interpreted is, God with us" (Matt. 1:23).

Throughout history there have been thrilling names, names to be admired. We think of such names as Abraham, Moses, David, Solomon, Isaiah, Daniel, Peter, James, and John. We think of Demosthenes, Cicero, Dante, Tennyson, and Milton. We think of Robert E. Lee, Stonewall Jackson, George Washington, and Woodrow Wilson. We think of the immortal Gladstone, George Whitefield, Jonathan Edwards, Henry Ward Beecher, and George W. Truett. We think of Alexander the Great, Caesar, Napoleon, and Churchill. How mighty and influential the names of history have been!

Yet, as great as they are, none of these names is so great as to equal the name of Jesus. None can be compared because Jesus stands alone — unique, august, supreme. With him no mortals among the sons of man can compare.

It is reported that Napoleon once said, "I know men, and I tell you that Jesus is not a man." He is truly a being apart.

Charles Lamb said that if there were a gathering of the most illustrious men of literature, and Shakespeare were to walk into their midst, they would all rise to do him honor; but that if Jesus Christ were to walk into the room, they would all immediately fall down on their knees.

As sweet and tender as the word mother is, there is a word even more beautiful. As beautiful as is the name wife, husband, son, or daughter, there is no name as sweet as the name of a Galilean peasant who died on the cross, was buried and rose again. Here, my friends, is an exalted name.

We date our letters by his name. His name is at the top of every important legal document. Every check bears his name. We measure time by Jesus; every time we look at a clock or calendar we are reminded of his birth.

"Wherefore God also hath exalted him."

An All-Powerful Name

Jesus' name is not only an exalted name; it is also an omnipotent, almighty, all-powerful name. Every knee should bow and every tongue confess that he is Lord. This means that Jesus reigns; he rules; he governs; he controls. At the very mention of his name, angels in heaven fall prostrate at his feet. Archangels sing praises to his name. Below the earth the devils cringe in fear and flee at the mention of his all-conquering name. They are tormented at the touch of his victorious hand. On earth he is the Lord of lords and King of kings. Every man is destined to bow to his name, and the kingdoms of this earth are destined to become the kingdoms of God. The glorious prophecy that all the glory of the Lord shall cover the earth as the waters cover the sea will someday be fulfilled. Jesus reigns. He must reign. He will reign until the last enemy has been put under his feet. We sing the words of Isaac Watts:

> Jesus shall reign where'er the sun
> Does his successive journeys run.

When I was a boy, I heard Billy Sunday say that people are going to hell by the carloads. Many would like to know how many will be saved and how many will be lost. In a pastorate I once had was a lovely woman who often told me that if God were to offer the same proposition that he had offered to Abraham long ago, no one would be able to find five righteous men in that town. Sometimes I wonder whether there are more people lost than saved. Then I hear Jesus say: "What is that to thee? Follow thou me."

Surely the world presents a dismal picture. Certainly the devil is powerful. But, my friends, I cannot believe that he is more powerful than Jesus Christ. There is a day of judgment coming, when every man shall give an account unto God for deeds done in the flesh. Every knee shall bow and every tongue shall confess. In Matthew 25 we are told that when God has the whole world before him, he is going to say to the sheep on the one hand, "Come, ye blessed of my Father, inherit the kingdom prepared for you . . . : for I was an hungred, and ye gave me meat: I was thirsty, and ye gave me drink: . . . I was sick, and ye visited me: I was in prison, and ye came unto me" (vv. 34-36). Then he's going to say to the goats, "Depart from me, ye cursed, into everlasting fire, prepared for the devil and his angels" (v. 41). Then it's going to be everlastingly too late. The saddest thing I can imagine is to stand in the judgment seat and hear Jesus have to say this to some person who had an opportunity to accept him and yet rejected him.

But I bring you good news. You do not have to hear Jesus say this because you're alive; you're in good health. You're able to worship, to hear God's Word. No matter how far you've gone in sin Jesus can heal you. His power can make you what you ought to be.

A sailor on a restless sea was cast out into the waters. To save himself he grabbed hold of a plank. Sometimes the waves swept over him; sometimes he rode the waves. Finally he was dashed ashore. His body was found and he was taken to a hospital. A minister came to visit him and asked if he were a Christian. The sailor replied, "No, I'm not a Christian. I've never been able to understand the meaning of salvation; it's too deep for me." Then the good minister said, "What happened to you when you were thrown overboard?" He explained that he had grabbed an old wooden plank. The minister said, "Well, that's it. Jesus is like a mighty plank in the midst of an ocean. He will never let you go." Twenty years later the minister met up with the sailor, and the sailor said, "I still have hold of the plank, and it bears."

It does bear, my friends. Jesus is a wonderful Savior. A poet has said:

I know of a land that is sunk in shame,
Of hearts that faint and tire;
But I know a name, a name, a name,
That can set that land on fire.

I know of a life all steeped in sin,
That no man's art can cure;
But I know a name, a name, a name,
That can make that life all pure.

I know of a soul that is lost to God,
Bowed down by things of earth;
But I know of a name, a name, a name,
That can give that soul new birth.

So listen, my heart, an angel speaks,
To save thy life from dross;
Christ Jesus is the name, the name,
He saves by way of the cross.

More than a century ago sweet Jenny Lind gave a farewell concert to the people of America in the great city of Washington. The President of the United States was there; members of both houses of Congress were present; members of the President's cabinet, representatives of the Army, Navy, and diplomatic corps, many governors, and many of the great and illustrious people of our nation attended to hear Jenny Lind sing. She had never sung more beautifully, and she was encored time and time again.

Finally, it became necessary for her to sing her farewell number. She glanced up in recognition of the ovation which she had received, and way above the audience she saw a lone figure, a man whose heart broke to give his song to the world. That man was John Howard Payne. She began singing this beautiful song:

Though through pleasure-filled palaces we may roam,
Be it ever so humble, there's no place like home.

It was whispered through the audience that John Howard Payne sat above this vast audience. Many of the people wept. The news reached the President, and we are told that there were tears in his eyes as he — and the rest of the audience — stood to their feet in honor of him whose heart broke to give his song to the world.

I do not know how true this story is, but I do know that while the mighty names of people of this earth have been magnified and glorified, Jesus Christ — whose name is above every name, who came and suffered and bled and died to redeem us from our sins, who left this earth to prepare a home for us — has looked down upon us from above. In honoring the names of the great and mighty of this earth, let us not forget to give honor to the name of him whose name is above all others. Let us say with the song:

> All hail the power of Jesus' name!
> Let angels prostrate fall;
> Bring forth the royal diadem,
> And crown Him Lord of all!

12. What's So Special About Jesus?

MATTHEW 16:13-16

"Thou art the Christ, the Son of the living God" (v. 16).

Some years ago I had the privilege of going to Spain on a preaching mission for the United States Air Force. When I was in Madrid, the chaplain there came one day and offered to show me some of the scenery surrounding the city. A sergeant drove us about thirty miles out of Madrid. The mountains were beautiful, and on top of one I could see a gigantic cross. They told me it is so large that two automobiles can pass each other on its arms. As we drew nearer, I could see that within the mountain which held the cross was a Roman Catholic cathedral. We walked up the steps, and entered through two huge doors into a magnificent cathedral. Candles were burning, the lights were dim, and beautiful music was playing. Inside and out were graves, for this was the Valley of the Fallen.

As we walked around, this young sergeant pointed out the grave of Spain's greatest martyr. Then we proceeded to the nave of the cathedral, where there was a rail around a large golden crucifix. On the cross hung the body of Jesus.

The young sergeant whispered in my ear, "There's supposed to be something very special about that Jesus up there." I told him that I did not know what might be special about that particular image, but I did know that there is a great deal special about Jesus himself. If Jesus had been only a martyr and a hero, he might have been in one of those graves. But he is more than any martyr, more than any mere hero; he is the

Savior from sin. He died on the cross to take away our sins, and yes, there is something very, very special about him.

Many people have raised the question, What's so special about Jesus? Many of our young people today are asking, for we are living in a speculative, philosophical, inquiring age. It is good that people are asking such questions as, Who is Jesus? Is he alive? Does he love us? Does he exercise any power in our lives, or is this story about Jesus a myth? Is it only the story of a good Jew who lived a good life and died and went to his grave? Is that all there is to this Jesus?

These questions have been asked not only by perplexed theological students but even theological professors. One day Jesus himself asked his disciples, "Whom do men say that I the Son of man am? And they said, Some say that thou art John the Baptist: some, Elias; and others, Jeremias, or one of the prophets. He saith unto them, But whom say ye that I am? And Simon Peter answered and said, Thou art the Christ, the Son of the living God" (Matt. 16:13-16). Jesus was very pleased with Peter's answer, and pronounced a spiritual benediction on him for his insight: "Blessed art thou, Simon Barjona: for flesh and blood hath not revealed it unto thee, but my Father which is in heaven" (v. 17).

The High View of Jesus

Ever since Jesus came into this world there have been two views regarding him: the low view and the high view, the right and the wrong view, the easy and the hard view. The low view of Jesus is that Jesus was a man — noble, wise, and good — the flower of the human race. But he was only a man: a man like Moses and David and Solomon; a man like James and John and Peter; a man like Thomas Aquinas, Martin Luther, and George Truett, but only a man.

The high view of Jesus is that he was all of this and more. He was the Son of man, but he was also the Son of God.

Strong Son of God, immortal Love,
Whom we, that have not seen thy face,
By faith, and faith alone, embrace.

The great God-man — the perfect merger of everything divine and everything human.

I say to you, my friends, that I hold to this high view of Jesus, for there is something special about him. There are four reasons why I hold to this view.

His Friends' Opinion

The first reason is what his best friends thought of him. If you want to know anything about a man, go back to his hometown and ask some of the people who knew him as a child what they think of him. They'll tell you. Don't think they won't! They know about him, and they'll tell people what they think. Let us ask the people with whom Jesus grew up — the people who knew him best, his contemporaries, his friends — what they thought of him.

Let us ask a man by the name of Matthew, who wrote a Gospel and painted a picture of Jesus as the fulfilment of all the Old Testament prophecy regarding the coming of the Messiah. He says that Jesus is the Messiah, the Son of God, the Savior of the world.

Let us ask a man by the name of John Mark, who saw Jesus at firsthand and in whose home Jesus visited. John Mark wrote a Gospel that paints a picture of Jesus as a wonder worker, a miracle worker.

Let us ask a man by the name of Luke who wrote the fullest and most complete of all the Gospels. In his book he tells us that Christianity is supreme because of who Jesus is; more than man, he is God in human flesh.

Let us ask a man by the name of John, who leaned upon the Master's breast. In his metaphysical and spiritual Gospel he tells us that "in the beginning was the Word, and the Word was with God, and the Word was God" (1:1). He says that Jesus was light and love and life.

Let us ask a man by the name of Paul of Tarsus, a great intellectual. When he speaks of Jesus, he speaks of Jesus as God.

Let us ask the author of the mysterious book of Revelation, a book of bloodshed and war, dragons and symbols. In the midst of many things we do not understand, there is one thing that is very clear: Jesus Christ is the Lamb of God who takes away the sins of the world.

These men who knew Jesus did not lie. When we hear "home folks" talk about who Jesus is, we can believe what they say. I cling to the high view of Jesus because I respect their opinions and judgment.

His Own Opinion

There is a second reason why I hold to this exalted view, and that is what Jesus says about himself.

Philosophers had long debated what is the way to life. Jesus said, "I am the way" (John 14:6). Walk ye in it.

They had long debated what life is. Jesus said, "I am . . . the life" (14:6). "I am come that [ye] might have life, and that [ye] might have it more abundantly" (10:10).

Philosophers had long debated what is the truth. Jesus said, "I am . . . the truth" (14:6) — all the truth you need to know.

He made some other colossal claims for himself. He said, "I am the light of the world: he that followeth me shall not walk in darkness" (8:12).

He said, "I am the bread of life: he that cometh to me shall never hunger" (6:35).

He said, "I am the good shepherd: the good shepherd giveth his life for the sheep" (10:11).

He said, "I am the door: by me if any man enter in, he shall be saved" (v. 9).

He said, "I am the resurrection, and the life: he that believeth in me, though he were dead, yet shall he live" (11:25).

He said, "I and my Father are one. No man cometh unto the Father, but by me. If ye had known me, ye should have known my Father also" (10:30; 14:6-7).

He said, "Come unto me, all ye that labour and are heavy laden, and I will give you rest" (Matt. 11:28).

He said, "The Son of man is come to seek and to save that which was lost. The Son of man came not to be ministered unto, but to minister, and to give his life a ransom for many" (Luke 19:10; Matt. 20:28).

Jesus knew what was involved in making divine claims for himself. He knew that to claim to be God and not to *be* God would be the rankest blasphemy. But if we take these claims of Jesus Christ and try to fit them on the brow of any other man who ever lived in all of history, they simply do not fit. Only upon the sacred brow of Jesus Christ do they fit with absolute perfection.

History's Opinion

A third reason I hold to this high view of Jesus is what history says about him. If we were measuring a period of one year, or ten years, or twenty years, and asking what history has said, we wouldn't have much to go on. But after twenty centuries! Is there any unanimity in what two thousand years of history says about Jesus Christ? Yes, there is. History proclaims him as the Son of God! Wherever the glorious gospel of Christ has gone, it has been the power of God unto salvation for all who believe.

A missionary has told the story of how some cannibals came one day into a little village in China and told the people to get off the streets and go home. To make sure that the people understood what they were talking about, they killed two or three children. Frightened, of course, the people did go home. But the missionary was not afraid. He went down to his little chapel and turned on the lights, and when they came in and threatened to kill him, he opened God's Word and began to read the story of how Christ loved us and bled on the cross for us. Their hearts mellowed, and thirteen of them accepted Jesus Christ as Lord and Savior. And until today, some of those men are fine Christians in China.

That is what the gospel has done around the world.

Samuel H. Hadley was a drunken bum. But he said, "If I ever become such a sot that I can't buy my own liquor, I'll jump in the Hudson River and end it all." One day he sat by a stove in a saloon in Harlem, stupefied with liquor, and someone said to him, "Now's the time to drown yourself. You're no good." Something came over Hadley, a power he couldn't understand. He walked up to the bar, pounded it with his fist, and said to the saloon keeper, "I'll never take another drop of liquor as long as I live." He walked out, suffered delirium tremens, went to jail for three days, and came out so weak he could hardly walk. He went to the Jerry M'Auley Mission in New York City, and heard people thanking God on their knees that they'd been saved from a life of drunkenness and sin. He heard Jerry and Mrs. M'Auley pray, and he fell down on his knees and said, "Oh, Lord Jesus, if you can help a poor old drunken bum like me, won't you please do it now?" And the burden of his soul rolled away. Samuel Hadley became a new man in Christ and the superintendent of that mission for twenty-five years.

This story could be multiplied a billionfold around the world, for wherever the gospel has been preached, it has changed the lives of men and women, boys and girls. As deep responds to deep, so does Jesus Christ respond to the words of each soul.

To the artist he is the ideal portrait.

To the astronomer he is the bright and morning star.

To the banker he is the hidden treasure.

To the biologist he is life.

To the carpenter he is the door.

To the doctor he is the Great Physician.

To the educator he is the Master Teacher.

To the farmer he is the seed of righteousness and Lord of the harvest.

To the florist he is the lily of the valley and the rose of Sharon.

To the geologist he is the Rock of ages.

To the horticulturist he is the true vine.

To the jeweler he is the pearl of great price.

To the judge he is the supreme judge of mankind.

To the juror he is the faithful and true witness.

To the lawyer he is the good advocate.

To the newspaperman he is good tidings of great joy.

To the architect he is the light of the world.

To the philanthropist he is the unspeakable gift.

To the preacher he is the Word of God.

To the railroad man he is the new and living way.

To the sculptor he is the living stone.

To the soldier he is the captain of salvation.

To the sailor he is the pilot across life's tempestuous sea.

To the poor sinner he is the Lamb of God who takes away the sin of the world.

Jesus Christ is all of this and ten million times more. No man can ever tell what Jesus is. He is more than any of us can ever say of him. That is why I believe there is something very, very special about Jesus.

A Final Reason

There is another reason I cling to the high view of Jesus, and that is what he has done for me. I once was a poor lost sinner. To be separated from God in your sins is to suffer the worst misery, to endure the blackest night that it is possible to endure. When I was told the story of God's love for me, I made up my mind to take Jesus at his word, commit my life to him, and follow him.

Jesus has done so much for me. How grateful I am that he saved my soul from sin! Many times I have felt like Gypsy Smith, the son of an ignorant nomad, who used to come home from his great revival crusades in Wales, pick up a rusty old knife that had been his father's, and say, "Here's what I would have been had it not been for the grace of God."

What Jesus Christ has done for me, my friends, he's done for many others. Around the world there are multiplied millions of people who have come to know him as Savior and Lord. They have come out of the darkness into a marvelous light. They have been dead and been resurrected to new spiritual life. They have been blind and received their sight. They have been healed of the disease of sin, and they have joy and peace in their hearts because of what Jesus has done for them. They are new men and women in Christ.

Do I understand it? No, I do not understand it. There are many things I do not understand. I don't understand space travel. I don't understand how radio and television work. I don't understand how jet planes fly. I don't even understand electricity. But I have sense enough to know that if you push a light switch one way, you'll put the lights out. If you push it the other way, you'll put the lights back on. I'd be a fool — just because I don't understand electricity — to cut out all the lights and live in darkness.

No, I don't understand why God is so good to us or why he's given us such a wonderful plan of salvation, but I know he's done it. I believe it. I accept it by faith. It has worked in my life, and it can work in your life, too.

Just a few months after I arrived in my present pastorate, I found all kinds of problems. Oh, how heavy my heart got! I had thirteen problems at one time, and all of them seemed insoluble. My wife and I cried all night long on our knees to God one night to help us solve them.

God works in mysterious ways. One by one he blotted out every one of those problems. And though we have had thirteen more, and thirteen more, he has continued to solve them, one by one.

I shall never forget a wonderful, gray-haired old man who used to come by my study. He'd come in smiling and say: "Now, pastor, quit worrying. We're just having growing pains in this church. There's nothing for you to worry about. I love you, and I'm praying for you. Let's pray together."

One day I was called to the hospital and told that he had cancer and wouldn't live long. I went to see him every day, and one day he said: "Pastor, do you know what I'd like to do more than anything else if I could? I'd like to go back and teach my men's Bible class just one more time. Do you know what I'd tell them? I'd tell them that Jesus Christ is a wonderful Savior to live by and a wonderful Savior to die by."

There is something very special about a Savior who shows us how to live and how to die. And he will save us if we let him.